Raised Italian-American

Raised Italian-American

✦

Stories, Values and Traditions from the Italian Neighborhood

Joseph J. Bonocore

iUniverse, Inc.
New York Lincoln Shanghai

Raised Italian-American
Stories, Values and Traditions from the Italian Neighborhood

iUniverse books may be ordered through booksellers or by contacting:

iUniverse
2021 Pine Lake Road, Suite 100
Lincoln, NE 68512
www.iuniverse.com
1-800-Authors (1-800-288-4677)

ISBN-13: 978-0-595-35721-5 (pbk)
ISBN-13: 978-0-595-67264-6 (cloth)
ISBN-13: 978-0-595-80198-5 (ebk)
ISBN-10: 0-595-35721-0 (pbk)
ISBN-10: 0-595-67264-7 (cloth)
ISBN-10: 0-595-80198-6 (ebk)

Printed in the United States of America

I dedicate this book to my family. I have been married to my wife Phyllis for over 35 years. We shared the same experiences since she also grew up in the same neighborhood. Her strong support and undying devotion over the years has been a major contributor to any success that I may have achieved during my lifetime.

This book is also dedicated to my three children Joseph, Kristen, & Michael. Although they are grown now and have lives of their own, I continue to learn from them daily. Their strength, intellect, and durability know no bounds as they travel their way through this journey that we call life. I wish them "God Speed" as they continue their exciting passage in life.

Also, special dedication to my grandchildren who are beginning their life journey and my daughter-in-law Chele Bonocore. To date, I have only been introduced to two of my grandchildren, Dominic and Isabella. I expect that as the years go by, more will appear. I hope that this book will shed some light on the experiences their grandfather had growing up and maybe some lessons that I learned along the way.

I also dedicate this book to my Mom and Dad. My father is no longer with us but Mom is as strong as ever. When I was a young boy, my mother would encourage me to do things that I did not want to do by saying the code that many Italian American immigrants lived by and why they found success in America: "Out of our habits grow our character on our character we build our destiny."

Contents

Preface

This is a story about the values and traditions of the Italian-American immigrants and how they taught these values and traditions to their children. It also is about the children of these immigrants, many of who became honorable citizens of the United States and made great contributions to this society.

The book also includes stories about my own experience of being raised Italian-American in South Philadelphia. These experiences are used as examples to illustrate some of the points made in the book, and, hopefully, keep you entertained along the way.

It was not hard for me to research the Italian-American history, traditions, superstitions, and organizations for this effort. But you might question how I determined the definition of Italian-American values. Well, it was not hard for me to define what the Italian-American values were at all. They were emphasized to me every day by my parents, my teachers, and every other responsible adult in my South Philadelphia neighborhood where I was raised.

They were discussed in basic terms like: "Get a good education or you will be forced to work as hard as your father" or "Value the freedom you have in this country, you could lose it at any time", or "You don't know what it is like in the old country". "Value your right to be free in a country where you can do what you want as an individual". Other values that my family emphasized included: "Family is forever" and "You should always protect your family." "The family bonds are sacred". "Idle hands are the devil's work shop". "You are lazy if you are not contributing to the family."

Some people will say that these values are not solely Italian-American. They are right. But I am writing this book from the point of view of how these values have been integrated into the Italian-American culture. I would encourage people from other cultures such as the Irish, Germans, and Jewish to write a similar book, if they have not already done so. It has been a very rewarding experience for me, a second generation, born in the United States Italian-American, to complete this project.

We start on this journey by discussing the large Italian migration to the United States from 1880 to 1920. We also present some of the ways that the early immigrant's lived as they earn a living in the new world. We review what they found when the arrived. We talk about the "Little Italy's" that were founded by the immigrants around the United States. We also discuss some of the discrimination that was experienced by the Italians in the New World upon their arrival.

The book explores the key role of the Catholic Church in building the Italian American neighborhoods. For example, we discuss the role that Bishop John Neumann played in building the Italian Catholic Parishes in South Philadelphia. We also discuss his leadership in building the elementary Catholic education system in Philadelphia in the mid 1800s. This became the foundation for the present Catholic elementary education system in the United States.

We analyze the role that early Italian-American organizations had in assisting the new immigrants in assimilating into the new country. These organizations include the Order of the Sons of Italy in America and The Italian Catholic Federation.

Our next step is to explain some of the Italian traditions and superstitions that the families used to bind themselves together in good times and in bad times. We explain holiday traditions such as those related to Easter, Christmas, and Valentines Day. Examples include the celebration of the Christmas Eve Feast of the Seven Fishes, the Nativity Scenes & how the family had home and church rituals around them, the tradition of LaBefana, cotechino con lenticchie on New Year's and many more.

We also discuss other traditions such as the tradition of naming new born children after relatives, making home made wine, the Italian formal wedding, the Italian funeral, the centuries-old tradition of street painting, and the South Philadelphia tradition of window dressing. We also explain a number of the Italian superstitions including the famous "Evil Eye" and the famous neighborhood Italian heath healers.

Our journey will then focus on eight key Italian-American values such as love of God and strong practice of faith, love of family, love of your country, caring for others who are less fortunate then ourselves, entrepreneurship and maintain the Italian heritage. In each area, we give examples of people and organizations that have or are applying these values to help in our society today.

In our examples, you will recognize many familiar names such as Rudy Giuliani, Joe Di Maggio, Lee Iacocco, Frank Capra, Vince Lombardi, Mario Puzo, Geraldine Ferraro, and Yogi Berra. However, I also have included examples of people who are not famous but are also excellent examples of these values as well. These include people such as Lido Iacocco (Lee's father), Sgt. John Basilone, Major Don Gentile, Dante Benedetti, Jimmy Martello, and Dominic Renzulli.

In the area of entrepreneurship, you will recognize some of the companies that we will use as examples that were founded by Italian-Americans including Tropicana, Planters Peanuts, and Hanna-Barbera Studio. However, we will also discuss some family owned companies that you may not know. Many of these companies have been in the same Italian-American family for 50 to 100 years or more.

In the last section, we will sum up by developing some "lessons learned" from our forefathers. It is no surprise that our neighborhoods today need some help. Our children are not growing up with the same set of values that they did in the past. Are there things that we can learn from our ancestors?

The idea to write this book came to me during the United States Presidential elections of 2004. During the election, there was a lot of talk about the importance that "Midwest values" played in the outcome of the election. The importance of hard work, committing your soul to Christ, devoting your life to the sanctity of marriage, and loving your neighbor as you loved yourself.

In fact, there are many communities in this country that do a great job in instilling these values in their children. One such community was where I was raised: South Philadelphia. Yes, "Little Italy" in Philadelphia was a great place to raise a family in the 1950's and 1960's. We were poor but each day, my parents, the teachers in my school, and the community organizations in the neighborhood emphasized love of God, love of family, love of your country, care for others who are less fortunate then yourself. And, they emphasized that in America, you had the freedom to be anything that you wanted to be if you work hard enough for it.

This does not say that these neighborhoods were an ideal place to live. In fact, it could be dangerous at times. There were gangs and crime. South Philadelphia was headquarters for the Philadelphia MAFIA as well as a number of very dangerous street gangs. There was a bad side of these neighborhoods.

What I intend to do is to show that despite all the crime, most of the families, churches, and local organizations reared many outstanding children who went on to live a good moral life. There are lessons to be learned from my community and others like it that raised these children.

I also wanted to write this book because so many of my Italian-American friends have lost sight of the Italian traditions. The traditions were such a rich part of my early years with my parents. They seem to be getting lost in history as we move further away from our roots. Many Italian-American adults that I know are looking for one place where they can go to reference some of the Italian traditions. My hope is that this book can fulfill that need. It can help the parents tell the story to their children of what it was like when they were growing up "in the neighborhood".

I am also writing this book for my children, my grandchildren, the parents, the teachers, the local officials and anyone who lives in the United States "neighborhoods" today. My hope is that after reading this book, they may reinstitute some of the appropriate ideas back into their families, their homes, their schools, and their churches and thus "rebuild some of these support institutions back into their neighborhoods for the sake of the future of their kids".

I understand that times have changed and these neighborhoods and the institutions and organizations that taught these values are slowly disappearing. The Italian-American neighborhood will probably disappear in the near future. My hope is that we can learn lessons from these immigrants and build a new Multi-Cultural neighborhood that preserves the same values of love of God, love of family, love of your country, care for others who are less fortunate then yourself, and continue to have the freedom to be anything that you want to be if you work hard enough for it.

However, even in these multi-cultural neighborhoods, I hope we never lose sight of the need to teach our children about their ethnic heritage and customs. It is so important that they know about ancestors and their history.

With this idea in mind, I set out on my task. To write a book about the individuals, institutions, and organizations that helped grow our Italian-American neighborhoods. By documenting these activities, I expect to (1) inspire a new generation of young people to follow in their foot steps, (2) encourage local leaders to implement some of these ideas in their neighborhoods, and (3) demonstrate that not all values and faith are in the Midwest.

If you doubt the accuracy of any of these stories or the lessons learned from this book, there is an easy way to check my credibility. Ask any Italian-American who was raised in an Italian-American neighborhood. They will have similar stories to tell. I know we cannot go back again. I just hope that as you read this book, maybe you can think of new ideas of how we can rebuild some of the old infrastructure into your new neighborhoods to "reconnect" as a "neighborhood" again rather then a just a house to come home to sleep.

When we were asked where we lived in 1960's, we said "South Philly" not our address. Maybe that spirit can return someday to our new homes. As I finished my research, I left this assignment with a feeling of encouragement. While the old neighborhoods are shrinking and the Italian-Americans are moving to the suburbs, many of the Italian-American clubs and organizations are growing, and new organizations are being started.

There seems to be a revival of the Italian-American cultural in the United States supported by many of the organization mentioned in this book. I hope that in my small way, this book contributes to this revival.

This book is for those 26 million Italian-Americans who want to keep the Values and Traditions alive.

Acknowledgments

I would like to thank my wife Phyllis Bonocore for all her help in the production and proofreading of this manuscript. She worked long hours checking my work and producing this document. Thanks also to Dr. Barbara Bundy, Executive Director of the Center for the Pacific Rim at the University of San Francisco who reviewed this book and gave me significant insights that improved its' presentation greatly.

I also appreciate the assistance provided by Jeff and Kami Sterling and Dickson Buxton and my son Michael Bonocore for reviewing the document and scheduling interviews. Thanks also go to my wife Phyllis Bonocore, my father-in law Tony Donze and my brother Robert Bonocore for providing me with the pictures that were used in this book.

Thanks also to the many Italian-Americans who gave their time to be interviewed for this book. Their stories are the backbone of this manuscript and their contributions are appreciated.

PART I
Italian-American
Neighborhoods Builders

1

The Italian Immigrants

My grandfather immigrated to the United States in 1915 from Palermo, Sicily. Sicily is an island that is part of Italy. He arrived at Ellis Island and shortly made his way to Philadelphia and like a number of his countrymen he found his way to South Philadelphia which is the "Little Italy" of Philadelphia. He told me a number of times one of the famous jokes that were told by many of the immigrants who came to the United States:

"When I got here, I found out three things: first, the streets weren't paved with gold; second, they weren't paved at all; and third, I was expected to pave them."

He felt more comfortable in South Philadelphia then anywhere else in the United States since there were many of his Italians countrymen living there. He was one of the lucky ones and managed to get a job in a manufacturing plant in the neighborhood. However, his luck was short-lived.

World War I arrived and it changed everything. He was off to Europe as a member of the United States Army. Once the war was over and he returned to South Philadelphia, things were very different. The good news was he became an American citizen. However, his ties to his family in Italy and the "old country" were severed. I think it was because he felt that he had failed his family. He never made the money that he thought he was going to make in the "new world".

It was at that time that I realized that he came to America to earn money and return to Italy rather then to settle here in the United States and to begin a new life. When he arrived in this country, he never intended to actually stay here and become a U.S. citizen.

His intent was to make enough money so that some day he too could return home to buy the land that his family sharecropped and he could marry his sweetheart back home in Italy. He planned to be away for only a defined period of time in search for money for the family. It took him longer then he and his family expected and they were angry with him for staying so long. He therefore broke all ties with his family in Italy because my grandfather had failed them.

Imagine, being told after all these years, that I am in the United States by accident and not by choice. My grandfather's original plan was to return to Italy and not to make a new life for himself in America.

Not only that, he assured me, most of the other single young Italian men, who also came over to United States with him had the same idea, i.e. to return to Italy. Their plans just changed because it was more difficult to make money then they thought and they did not have the money to return or, after they got their feet on the ground, they changed their mind and brought their relatives to the United States.

So, like my grandfather, Antonio Bonocore, many of them decided to make a life for themselves in the United States as best as they could. Antonio chose South Philadelphia. Others chose cities like New York, Boston, Chicago, Cleveland and Pittsburgh.

The rest was history for him and the other immigrants that came to America with him. That is the subject of this book.

When my grandfather and the other 4,481,416 Italians arrived in the United States, during the period between 1880 and 1924, they may be responsible for one of the largest exoduses in history. It must have been an amazing sight as they streamed through the traditional ports of immigration at Castle Garden and later at Ellis Island in New York harbor.

As they walked through the station being processed into the United States, pinned to their lapels, blouses and shirts were cards with their names, destinations and the familiar "W.O.P.", an abbreviation for "Without Papers." It has now taken a more derogatory meaning, but then it indicated only the hurried circumstances of immigration.

History tells us that the main reason for any immigration is economic opportunity, i.e. the lure of better land or a better job. For example, the rich prairie land of the United States was the attraction for the many farmers from Europe in the 1880s. History also tells us that immigration in the United States took place in waves.

The first wave (1600 to the 1820's) began with the colonist and it reached its' peak before the Revolutionary War. Most of these early colonists came from England. The second wave (1820 to the 1870's) lasted until a depression in the early 1870s. Most of these immigrants came to the United States from northern and western Europe. About 1/3 of these immigrants were Irish and settled on the east coast. Many were Germans who had enough money to venture inland and settled on farms of the Midwest.

The third wave started around 1870 and continued until 1960. By the early 1880's, Immigration patterns had changed. The United States economy suffered a depression while the economies of Germany and Britain improved significantly. Therefore, immigration from Germany and Britain declined but immigration increased from other countries like Norway, Sweden, Denmark, and Southern and Eastern Europe including Italy.

Italian immigration to the United States never happened in large numbers until the 1880s. One reason for this is that Italy never colonized the United States earlier like Spain, England, and France did. The vast majority of the Italian immigrants came from southern Italy where economic hardship forced them to look for other places to help them provide livelihood for themselves and their families.

Most of these immigrants passed through New York and Ellis Island and they settled in New York City or other large cities in the North East part of the United States. However, these were not the first Italians to travel to American. Several Italian explorers ventured to America well before they did.

A Genoese sailor, Cristoforo Colombo, or Christopher Columbus, was one of the most famous Italians to reach the New World when he discovered America in 1492. Other Italian explorers who traveled to the America included John Cabot (Giovanni Caboto), Giovanni da Verrazano, and Amerigo Vespucci. Later, in the late 1700s, a small group of northern Italians immigrated to America. They were mainly skilled artisans, painters, sculptors, musicians, and dancers. Also, periodically, political refugees came to America, fleeing the failed liberal revolutions of the early nineteenth century. The most famous of these was Giuseppe Garibaldi.

However, this early Italian migration lacked significant numbers to make a large impact on the American culture at the time. But, their settlement provided a base from which a later mass migration was to build.

THE GREAT ITALIAN MIGRATION (1880-1925)

By the beginning of the Great Italian Migration, only 1,862 Italian immigrants had made homes in New York City, but by the time of the great migration, the city was to become the home to millions of Italians. Many Italians justified their migration with an old proverb that would surely influence new emigrants: "Chi esce riesce (He who leaves succeeds)." In 1850, there were reportedly less then 4,000 Italians in the United States. By 1880, the Italian population was estimated at 44,000 and by 1900 to 484,027. According to the 2000 United States census, 26 million American say they are Italian Americans.

The surge of the Italian exodus began after the Italian unification during the Risorgimento of 1860-1870. The urban north prospered from a united Italy but the economically poor south did not. Italy became a nation very late compared to other European countries. Italy has a history of fragmented independent regions, diverse dialects and isolated hill-towns. It also has a history of a number of foreign invasions and of warring between each of its regions.

The first phase of the great migration was primarily men moving to the United States. They sought a temporary home. They wanted to make money and then return home to their families and friends. The first immigrants were usually males fifteen to thirty-five years of age, who traveled into the large Northeast American cities looking for work. However, statistics show, almost half of these immigrants returned to Italy and their *paese* (village) from which they came.

In the next phase of the migration, after 1910, women and entire families began to immigrate to the United States. Most of these Italian immigrants passed through Ellis Island, and at this time more Italians resided in New York City than in the Italian cities of Florence, Venice, and Genoa combined. The Italian immigrant was very reliant on the *padrone*. The *padrone* (labor boss) found work for these new immigrants, usually securing jobs for the Italians on his arrival to American. Typically, the immigrants found work as industrial laborers, long-shoremen or construction workers.

As the second generation of Italians was born, they became more American-ized. Discrimination toward the Italians lessened over time as more Italian-Amer-icans fought in World War I and World War II. In many situations, education was provided for the Italian immigrants by the Catholic Church through the parochial schools that were established in neighborhoods. The Italian families were torn between the opportunity to have their children educated by the church and the need to have the children go to work to help the family survive.

Over time, education and professional training helped raise the position of the Italian-Americans in the United States society. While they have assimilated well into the American society, today's Italian Americans retain many of the traits that they brought with them from the "old country" like family loyalty and many are still geographically concentrated in the same areas as their forefathers.

The immigrants were very confused by the new language. In Italian *ben edu-cato* meant well-mannered, but in English "well-educated" referred to the num-ber of years of schooling one had.

By the second generation, Italian Americans were interested in having their children educated and encouraged their children to get an education. The second generation also discouraged spoken Italian and ethnic customs in favor of Ameri-can ones thinking that it would provide more opportunities for their children.

ITALIAN IMMIGRANTS WAY OF LIFE

Many of the immigrants of this period came to America as sojourners seeking employment, and they planned to stay only as long as it took to earn what was needed to return to Italy. In the first wave of the immigrant's arrival in the United States, many Italian's migrated as seasonal laborers. Some of these immi-grants were referred to as "birds of passage," and were assisted by *padrones* (labor agents) in finding employment and living accommodations.

The *padrone* was a phenomenon peculiar to the Italian community. He was a middleman who acted, sometimes unscrupulously, as an interpreter, employment agent, banker, and lawyer to the immigrants. The non-English speaking newcomers found it very difficult to function in America without the *padrone* who overcharged for their services. The *padrone* was very helpful in finding jobs for immigrants, especially employment away from the eastern port cities.

The immigrants in the first wave were predominantly male who arrived without families. This meant separation from the Italian family and sometimes they were never reunited.

The Italians came to find work and not, as assumed, to find streets lined with gold. Work meant survival to these men who were leaving a home where they had no hope of finding a job there. Many who arrived in the United States frequently found that the jobs were already held by slave labor, freed blacks or Germans. Because their numbers were not great, the early arrivals found jobs with the railroad or opened boarding houses near the train station. Others went to work in shoe repair, as tailors, bricklayers and furniture makers.

When they arrived, they built railroads, tunneled under harbors, highways, and subway systems, extracted coals from mines, and worked in factories. They worked under the most primitive of conditions and against all odds and obstacles including a new language and culture, prejudice in the forms of ethnic slurs and negative stereotypes, even violence directed against them.

Other Italians that were agrarians by nature were attracted to the market area and they introduced new varieties of produce that they grew on their home plots. Many who came from an agrarian background found ways to raise produce wherever they settled. They would then peddle fruits and vegetables or became grocers. After the 1900's the migration consisted of more common laborers, many of who went to work in the factories and were paid between $1.00 and $1.50 per day.

Many times we hear stories that lead us to romanticize the opportunity the immigrants had in their journey to the United States but in reality it was a marginal existence at best. Their lives reflected a sense of loss of their homeland, the uncertainties of the choices they had made, and constant fears of hostility and discrimination.

My grandfather told me on many occasions that without the support of the family, his *paesani*, and the comfort of his religion, he would not have survived. I am sure that many of the early immigrants must have felt the same. On the other hand many Italian men could not make the cultural adjustment and returned to Italy for good. Others would be joined later by their wife and family to establish a permanent home in America.

My grandfather and others in South Philadelphia told me how they kept in contact with their families and friends in Italy during those early years. That formed an important link in what later became known as chain migration. The early immigrant's settlements could only afford inexpensive housing that was available near the factory that employed them and the population was dense around the factory. However, they set up their living patterns to retain their familiar Italian culture and to support of their *paesani*, much like what they left behind in Italy. Therefore one would find the Neapolitans on one street while the Calabrese settled on another.

As with most new immigrants to the United States, many Italian immigrants could not afford housing or to keep their children in school. This was compounded by the fact that many did not speak English and the Italian immigrants were often feared and ostracized.

The Italian women that did immigrate went to work in the garment factories or they took piecework into their homes. This was very different for many women. They would never have been allowed to work out of the home in Italy where they would be confined to the home and raising children. As in Italy, the family was a continuous theme in the Italian American community. A woman's first responsibility was to the needs of her family. She would never put herself first.

The church for the Italian-Americans was not just a place of worship. It replaced the unity of the old-world village where each village had its own patron saint. In America the Catholics brought with them their patron saints into their new communities and their new parishes. The role of the parish, like the role of the village, was to help strengthen families, educate children and take care of the poor. It was a center of both social and religious life.

The Italian Americans also formed mutual assistance Associations. These groups often formed along the lines of occupations. For instance, there was one for tailors and another for construction workers. These groups were like insurance agencies for the workers and they provided benefits for widows and for sick or injured persons.

My grandfather told me that long working hours allowed little time for more than gatherings for meals, picnics or an occasional card game in a neighborhood saloon. In South Philadelphia, the immigrants who belonged to mutual associations would attend monthly meetings and some associations sponsored social events.

ITALIAN DISCRIMINATION

In the early years, Italians experienced a significant amount of discrimination. In this section we will discuss two of the most famous cases. One of the cases happened in New Orleans and the other that happened in Boston.

One of the more famous cases is the largest lynching in United States history where eleven Italian Americans were lynched in New Orleans on March 14, 1891. During the mid to late 1800's a large number of Italians came to the United States and settled in New Orleans where there were many opportunities to work on the farms and in the fish markets. New Orleans had the largest population of Sicilians in the United States at this time.

The chief of police in New Orleans was a man by the name of David Hennessey. He was investigating the murder of a Sicilian immigrant which was the result of a family feud between two Sicilian families. Hennessey's investigation led him to this vendetta. The members of this Sicilian neighborhood felt that the chief was prying. The Sicilian families believed that the police were involved in a matter that was not any of their business. One night, the chief was murdered by a handful of assassins.

A dozen or more Sicilian immigrants were charged with his murder, beaten, tortured and thrown in jail. The Ambassador of Italy intervened calling the whole situation a great miscarriage of justice. The court dismissed all murder charges against the Italians. The people in New Orleans were enraged and demanded revenge when they heard the court's verdict. A mob of non-Italian citizens entered the market, knocking over tables, beating and clubbing innocent merchants, women and children. They proceeded to the jail where the suspects were still being held. The suspects were beaten, shot dead, lynched, hung in public and shot again.

President Harrison spoke out against the incident and arranged for Congress to award the families of the victims $25,000 each. It was wrong that the police chief was murdered for doing his job but the fact remains that the murder of Hennessey is unsolved to this day. All of the suspects, guilty or innocent, were lynched by a mob of upwards of twenty thousand people that day. There were many other Italian immigrants that were lynched in many states across the South and Midwest.

Another story about Italian discrimination happened in Boston in the 1920s where a shoe company paymaster and guard were robbed and murdered in broad daylight on South Braintree Street. The two robbers made off with $15,000. Witnesses said that the suspects looked Italian. Over the next few weeks, a large number of Italian immigrants were questioned. Two North Enders (the Italian section of Boston) were arrested. They were Nicola Sacco and Bartolomeo Vanzetti. Both men were known anarchists, who had protested American entry into WW I and had fled to Mexico to avoid conscription into the U.S. Army.

The main evidence against them at their trial was that they were both carrying guns when arrested on a Quincy streetcar. Both of the men had good alibis. Vanzetti was selling fish in Plymouth. Sacco was with his wife at the Italian Consulate in Boston having his passport photograph taken. The attorneys for the prosecution focused on the fact that those who testified in support of these alibis were also Italian immigrants. They pointed out the men's radical political beliefs, accusing them of unpatriotic behavior for having fled to Mexico to escape the draft. Sacco and Vanzetti were found guilty of first-degree murder and sentenced to death.

All their appeals were denied. There were numerous large public demonstrations in their defense across the United States and throughout Europe, South America and Japan. Sacco and Vanzetti were executed on August 23, 1927. Their wake was attended by over 100,000 mourners. The funeral procession attracted 50,000 marchers.

Eventually the Italians overcame this discrimination and many of the obstacles that came their way. Despite instances of discrimination and exploitation, the Italians did not surrender their values and culture. Instead, they developed religious, political, economic and social institutions to support them in adjusting their life and to preserve their heritage.

PROMINENT ITALIAN IMMIGRANTS TO THE UNITED STATES

But by no means were all the Italian immigrants that came to America poor and uneducated. In fact, many educated and skilled Italians immigrants came to this country and contributed immediately to America's growth and prosperity.

Some of those that significantly contributed to the economic; physical; and moral growth of our nation are discussed in this section of the book but there are many more that are not mentioned.

Piccirilli Brothers

Best known for carving the Lincoln Memorial in Washington, D.C., the six Piccirilli Brothers immigrated to New York City in 1867. All six were trained as sculptors. The Lincoln Memorial and many other well-known public sculptures were actually carved in the Piccirilli Brothers' 142nd street studio in the Mott Haven section of the Bronx. They carved numerous other artists' designs as well, including J.Q.A. Ward, A. Saint Guadens, and R.I. Aitken.

In the early 20th century, the Piccirillis were commissioned to work on such famous Manhattan landmarks as the Brooklyn Museum of Art, the New York Stock Exchange, the United States Custom House, the New York Public Library, and City Hall Park. These opportunities came about largely as a result of the national public recognition Attilio won for his work on the Maine Monument at Columbus Circle (on the southwest side of Central Park). By the 1930's the status of sculpture had changed, and commissions dwindled for the brothers.

Their studio complex (142nd St. between Willis and Brook Avenues), which had grown to four buildings during the course of their lives and included adjacent row houses, was demolished sometime during the 1960s. What happened to the documents and possessions contained within still remains a mystery.

Enrico Fermi

Time Magazine called Enrico Fermi "the last of the double-threat physicists: a genius at creating both esoteric theories and elegant experiments". Enrico was awarded the Nobel Prize for Physics in 1938. His theory of beta decay introduced the last of the four basic forces know in nature (gravity, electromagnetism, and operating within the nucleus of the atom, the strong force and Fermi's "weak force").

Enrico Fermi was born in Rome in 1901 and immigrated to the United Stated in the mid-30s with his family to escape the persecution in Mussolini's Italy. When Enrico won the award, the United States created the Enrico Fermi Award in the Department of Energy in his honor.

Mother Cabrini

In March of 1889, Mother Cabrini, arrived in New York from Italy and immediately visited Archbishop Corrigan and told him of her plans to start an orphanage. For twenty-eight years, she overcame many obstacles and was the founder of sixty-seven schools, hospitals, and missions, one for every year of her life.

Mother Cabrini was born Maria Francesca Cabrini on July 15, 1850. She was born in the town of San Angelo, south of Milan, Italy. She helped her parents work the farm until she founded the Missionary of Sisters of the Sacred Heart in 1880. In 1909 Mother Cabrini became a United States citizen and was beatified in 1938 and canonized a saint in 1946.

Franco Modigliani

Franco Modigliani, an Economist, arrived in New York in August of 1939, a few days before the beginning of World War II. He was here on a scholarship at the New School for Social Research to continue his studies and planned to work during the day to support his family while he studying at night. He was affiliated with such Universities as University of Chicago, University of Illinois, Carnegie

Institute of Technology (now Carnegie-Mellon University); and he was a visiting professor at MIT.

In the late 1960's he had a major responsibility for developing a large-scale model of the U.S. economy sponsored by the Federal Reserve Bank. Until he died, in 2003, he actively participated in the debate over economic polices both in Italy and the United States concentrating lately on the effects of the huge public deficits. In 1985, Franco won the Nobel Prize in Economics.

Franco was born in Rome. His father died when he was thirteen. According to Franco in his autobiography, "I suddenly realized how deeply I loved him and at 13 my whole world seemed to collapse". His Mother, his family, and his values pulled him through this time and made him one of the great Economic leaders of the century.

Rita Livi-Montalcini

Rita Livi-Montalcini won a Nobel Prize in Medicine in 1986. She was born in 1909 in Turin, Italy and received her medical degree from the University of Turin in 1936. Levin-Montalcini's research focused on the development of the vertebrate nervous system. With her colleague, Stanley Cohen, she was awarded the Nobel Prize in physiology or medicine in 1986 for the discoveries of NGF and epidermal growth factor.

In her autobiography, *In Praise of Imperfection, My Life and Work*, Rita Levi-Montalcini says that her father believed that "A professional career would interfere with the duties of a wife and a mother." Apparently she convinced her father differently.

Gian Carlo Menotti

Another Italian immigrant of note is Gian Carlo Menotti. He won the Pulitzer Prize for his first full-length work, *The Counsul*, and the New York Drama Critics Circle award as the best musical play of the year in 1954. His best know work is the Christmas classic *Amahl and the Night Visitors*, composed for NBC-TV in 1951. This beloved opera celebrated its 50th anniversary of its premiere in 2001

Carlo was born in Cadegliano, Italy on July 7, 1911. Upon the death of his father, his mother took him to the United States where he was enrolled at Philadelphia's Curtis Institute of Music. He completed his studies there under the Rosario Scalero, another prominent Italian musician.

Each of these represents examples of hundreds of men and women who arrived on the United States shores from Italy and contributed greatly to the country.

2

The Italian-American Neighborhoods They Built

Italian immigrants brought their family-centered culture to America, which resulted in their highly concentrated settlements or "Little Italies" When the immigrants arrived, they tended to live together on the same streets or areas in these heavily congested Northeast cities.

Immigrants also sought the protection of the "Little Italies" because of the hostility they faced in American society. Seemingly resistant to assimilation, the Italians were despised as a minority rooted in the working class, however, within the Little Italies new generations of Italian Americans were being born, and changes took place between society and the Italians. Unlike the Irish, the Jews, the Germans, or the Polish, who dispersed themselves in other immigrant groups, the Italians remained together in their own communities and to some extent even today.

For example, if you look at the distribution of the Italian American population in the United States today you will find that it is still very concentrated in a small number of States and a small number of Cities. This is very different from the Germans, for example, who are widely dispersed across the United States. By State, New York has the largest population of Italian-Americans followed by New Jersey, California, and Pennsylvania.

Italian Americans Living in the U.S. (1990 Census) By State

State	Italian Americans	% of Population
New York	2.9 million	16%
New Jersey	1.5 million	20%
California	1.5 million	5%
Pennsylvania	1.4 million	12%
Massachusetts	845,000	15%
Connecticut	630,000	20%
Rhode island	230,000	20%

New York City has the largest population of Italian-Americans. It is followed by Philadelphia, Chicago, and Boston.

Italian Americans Living in the U.S. (1990 Census) By City

Rank	City	Italian Population
1	New York	1,882,396
2	Philadelphia	497,158
3	Chicago	492,158
4	Boston	485,761
5	Pittsburgh	316,351
6	Los Angeles/ Long Beach	308, 409
7	Detroit	280,051
8	Cleveland	179,733
9	Rochester	170,910
10	Washington, DC	163,440

New York's "Little Italy"

Immigrants from Italy first settled in the Five Points neighborhood of New York City in the 1850s, spreading north into what is now Little Italy in the 1880s. The Five Points was New York's original and most notorious slum. Located at the southwest corner of what is now Columbus Park, which is a few blocks below Canal at Baxter Street. The district teemed with gangs, prostitutes, criminals and street urchins. Little Italy's Italian population peaked at 10,000 around 1910. It was like a self-contained village, with its own language, customs, and cultural institutions all its' own.

For years, it was a target for reformers of all stripes and was an embarrassment to civic planners. The dark and airless tenements of the Five Points were finally demolished in an early urban renewal effort. By the close of the nineteenth century, New York City had several Italian sections. Northern Italians settled in Greenwich Village and what is now Soho. Southern Italians, particularly Neapolitans, Sicilians and Calabrians settled in Little Italy. As with other Italian-American neighborhoods, the groups even lived together: Mulberry Street, for example, largely housed immigrants from Napoli, while Elizabeth Street housed Sicilians.

Some people claim that the first pizzeria in New York was Gennaro Lombardi's, which opened on Spring Street in 1905 and reopened in 1994 just down the street from its original location. Immigrants from southern Italy first celebrated the Feast of San Gennaro along Mulberry Street in about 1926.

A small but notorious minority of Italians formed crime syndicates modeled on secret societies in Italy. Some claim that this Little Italy may have been the birthplace of the Mafia in the United States. Today, Little Italy has about 50 or so restaurants and cafés and caters to tourists, covering a dense neighborhood of tenements shared by recent Chinese immigrants, young Americans who can't afford Soho, with a few remaining real live Italians.

This is the neighborhood where Crazy Joe Gallo earned his nickname by walked the streets with a lion on a leash, and John Gotti held court outside the Ravenite Social Club.

Most Precious Blood Parish, located in the heart of "Little Italy" NYC, was founded by the Scalabrini Fathers in the 1888 to minister to the Immigrant

Catholic Italians. Staffed by the Franciscan Friars since 1892, it continues to minister to the needs of the Italian population and the many visitors and tourists to Little Italy.

Boston's North End

The first Italian immigrants came to the North End in the 1860s from Genoa and settled in a three-block area off Fulton Street, adjacent to the Jewish Menorah Products poultry slaughterhouse. They numbered fewer than 200. The Genoese were followed by the Campanians, who were followed by the Sicilians, the Avellinese, the Neopolitans, and the Abruzzesians. Each group settled in their own area within the North End, creating their own area within the greater North End neighborhood

After they began to arrive, the Protestant churches were acquired by the Catholic Archdiocese of Boston. For example, The Seaman's Bethel Church became the Sacred Heart Church in 1871 after Rev. Edward Taylor's death. St. Leonard's was completed in 1899 becoming the first Italian church in New England and the second oldest in America.

By 1900, the Italian population in the North End was 14,000. Over the next 20 years it would more than double to 37,000 and at its peak, in 1930, 44,000 Italians were packed into an area less than one square mile in size. The first arrivals, the Genoese, made their living as fruit and vegetable vendors and as peddlers selling wine, cheese, and olive oil from North End storefronts and from stalls along the open air Haymarket in Dock Square

The Sicilian immigrants, who had colonized the length of North Street along the harbor by 1925, found employment in the booming commercial fishing fleets. Others were able to find work in the construction trades—as masons, metalworkers, carpenters, and general laborers—with Italian owned and operated contractors.

In 1920, the North End had 28 Italian physicians, six Italian dentists, eight funeral homes, and along just one block of Hanover street four or five barbershops. Most North End businesses were of the "Ma and Pa" variety—small grocery stores, butcher shops, and bakeries, dressmakers, cobblers and shoe stores.

"Big & Little Italy' in Cleveland

The 1870 census listed 35 Italians in Cleveland. According to that census, these Italians were employed in mining, manufacturing, steelwork, and boot making, and as stone masons, about half of all Italians migrating to Cleveland moved from only 10 villages in southern Italy. The major Italian districts and cities that they came from were Patti and Palermo in Sicily, Benevento in the Campania and Campobasso in the Abruzzi. Together, these regions provided about 70% of the Italians coming to Cleveland.

The first Italian community in Cleveland was commonly known as Big Italy and was located along Woodland Avenue from Ontario and Orange Avenues to East 40th Street. At the turn of the century this section was populated by about 93% Sicilians and was the center of the city's produce markets.

In the decade ending in 1930 the Italian population recorded in the census tracts as living in "Big Italy" fell from 4074 Italian-born in 1920 to 2063 in 1930. More Italians were coming into Cleveland but they no longer lived in this original settlement. By 1940 only about 1300 Italians remained in "Big Italy." The second major Italian settlement in Cleveland was "Little Italy" located from East 119th to East 125th Streets on Murray Hill and Mayfield Roads. In 1911 it was estimated that 96% of the population of this neighborhood was Italian-born.

Many of these Italians in Little Italy were Neapolitan and were engaged in skilled lacework, the embroidery trades and garment making. The largest district group in "Little Italy" came from the towns of Ripamolisano, Madrice and San Giovanni in Galdo, which are in the province of Campobasso, in the region known as the Abruzzi.

"Little Italy" in Baltimore

Little Italy in Baltimore encompasses about 12 square blocks bounded on the north by Pratt Street, the south by the Harbor, the east by Eden Street and the West by President Street. The Italian immigrants arrived by ship or by train from New York where ships had taken them to Ellis Island. The trains emptied their passengers in Baltimore at the station on President Street, which was as close to Little Italy as the Harbor.

Later concentrations of Italians settled in the market areas of Lexington, Hanover, Belair and Cross Streets. The Catholic Church on the east coast in the early 19th century reflected its Irish roots. Italians did not feel at home with the more subdued form of worship and the priests felt that some of the Italian rituals were too flamboyant.

As a result, in 1881, St. Leo de Magno was established in the heart of Little Italy. In 1917, the second parish, St. John the Baptist, was formed in the Italian market community of Lexington. The year, 1923, saw the creation of yet a third parish, Our Lady of Pompeii, which was the center of the Highlandtown Italian community.

North Beach, CA.

San Francisco's North Beach neighborhood, also known as Little Italy, is situated between Chinatown and Fisherman's Wharf with Telegraph Hill and Coit Tower on the east and Russian hill on the west. Italian immigrants who came from the coastal fishing villages along the gulf of Genova and the Ligurian sea found that California gave them an opportunity to continue doing what they had been doing for a living in Italy, that is to fish.

The first settlement of Italian fishermen in California was in the San Francisco bay area. As early as 1870 Italian fishermen were providing ninety percent of all fish consumed in San Francisco. Some of San Francisco's Italian fishermen migrated south around 1871 and settled in what is now known as the Little Italy neighborhood in San Diego.

Italian immigration was very targeted by region in the United States. For example, four Italian provinces supplied most of the emigrants to San Francisco. These provinces were Genoa, Lucca, Cosenza, and Palermo. Emigrants from Genoa and Palermo were familiar with trade businesses or industrial skills and others were vine growers. These were skills all needed in the Bay Area at that time. North Beach is a somewhat compact layout of three-story buildings painted in light colors dating from the 1920s when people rebuilt after the earthquake and fire of 1906.

Joe DiMaggio, whose father was a fisherman, moved to North Beach at the age of one and lived at Valparaiso and Taylor.

"Little Italy" in Portland, Oregon

In the late 1800's Italians immigrated to Portland to build a better life. As the Italian population increased, the first Little Italy in Portland came together around Front Ave. through Fourth Street. The first Italian Boarding House was located on Front Ave. New immigrants coming into Portland were told to go to Garibaldi's Market to be given work at the railroads and other places. Italians worked hard and played hard. They worked on the surrounding farms and sold goods at the local markets, including the well-known Yamhill Marketplace. In 1920, the local Italian Gardener's Association was formed.

St Michael's church is still in use on Fourth and SW Mill and was known to be the "Italian Church." The church included an elementary school. Now those students are still Portland residents that tell creative stories with fond memories of the past. Much of the history of Italians in Portland is recorded at the Oregon Historical Society.

In the 1980's another flow of Italian immigrants arrived in Portland, bringing new life to the Italian-American community. This new group of immigrants has created a new resurgence of Italian vitality. New activities have come alive, such as the annual "Festa Italiana" that draws over 100,000 people in Pioneer Square each year.

Bensonhurst, Brooklyn, NY

Bensonhurst is a neighborhood located in the south-central part of New York City's borough of Brooklyn. In the early 1900s, many Italian immigrants moved into the neighborhood, and today their descendants make up the vast majority of its population.

Its main thoroughfare, 86th Street between roughly 14th Avenue and Stillwell Avenue, is lined with predominantly small, family-owned businesses, many of which have remained in the same family for several generations, and is topped by an elevated subway line. Visitors from throughout the New York City metropolitan area return to the neighborhood each year in late August or early September to take part in the colorful Santa Rosalia Festival, which actually falls on September 4, but the festival itself is often held over the Labor Day weekend for purposes of convenience.

St. Rosalia is the patron saint of the city of Palermo and is sometimes venerated as the patron for the entire island of Sicily (a large proportion of Bensonhurst's Italian American residents claim Sicilian heritage).

On August 23, 1989, the neighborhood made national headlines when Yusef Hawkins, a 16-year-old African American, went there with three of his friends to inquire about a used car which was for sale, only to be set upon by an angry mob of youth from the neighborhood, one of whom, armed with a handgun, shot Hawkins, causing his death. Spike Lee's film Jungle Fever is dedicated in memory of Hawkins.

Bensonhurst is named after Egbert Benson (1746-1833), New York State's first Attorney General following the Revolutionary War

"Little Italy" Willington, Delaware

Between 1880 and 1920, a wave of "new immigration" came to Delaware from southern Italy. They came to work as contract laborers on the railroad and to work as builders. By 1890, there were 459 Italian-born residents in Delaware, and their numbers grew by the close of the century.

The leather, iron, and steel industries in Delaware attracted Italian immigrants who wanted a better life. As with other cities, many of the early immigrants were men who left their families behind temporarily until they could establish themselves and bring their families to Delaware. They often stayed in boarding houses with other workers. Eventually, they brought families to Willington and bought homes.

Over the years, these immigrants settled in the neighborhood around Union and Lincoln Streets between Pennsylvania and Lancaster Avenues. They brought with them a strong, determined and independent culture, which they preserved through strong family structures and ties. The neighborhood was first known as "The Hill," and eventually "Little Italy."

As Italian immigrants continued to settle in Delaware many began to open their own businesses, such as "mom and pop shops." They opened fruit stores and offered their services as shoemakers, tailors, barbers, bakers, butchers, and cheese and macaroni makers. Later they became restaurateurs, grocery and other retail store operators.

"Little Italy" in Chicago

Italian immigrant first arrived in Chicago around 1850. Only 43 were counted in Illinois in that year's United States Census. But over time the number in Chicago grew and it now is the City with the third largest Italian-American population in the United States. Those who originally emigrated from Italy were mostly from southern Italy and Sicily, and encountered hardship and a negative stigma from their neighbors.

But the Italian community proved themselves to be an established presence over the years and in the heart of Chicago's near West Side, a dispersed but beautiful community still exists today. Our Lady of Pompeii Church was the first to open its doors in Little Italy in April of 1911. On October 10th, 1994, Joseph Cardinal Bernadin proclaimed the church a shrine, a center of hospitality, evangelization and spiritual growth founded in the Italian tradition and culture.

"Little Italy" in St. Louis

Settled in the early 1900s by Italian immigrants, residents still carry on their traditions in this lively neighborhood just minutes from downtown. The original Italian families who settled in St. Louis came from the town of Cuggiono, and from several other small Lombard villages clustered near Milan. They first came to the city of Herrin, Illinois to work in the coal mines in that part of southern Illinois known as "Little Egypt". This history is celebrated annually with a festival called HERRINFESTA ITALIANA.

The history of the Italian-American growth in St. Louis is an interesting one. It includes labor warfare, union strikes, religious tension between the Catholics and the Protestants, and the takeover by the Ku Klux Klan.

The neighborhood's fireplugs are painted green, white and red in tribute to the tri-color of the flag of Italy. Baseball stars Yogi Berra, Joe Garagiola and Jack Buck grew up on The Hill's Elizabeth Avenue, which now bears the name "Hall of Fame Place" in their honor. Neighbors still know everything about each other in this community of neat houses surrounded by tiny yards decorated with Blessed Virgin Mary statues.

"Little Italy" in San Diego

"Little Italy" in San Diego has been a stable ethnic business and residential community since the 1920's. "Little Italy" today represents Downtown San Diego's oldest continuous neighborhood business district. At one time, more than 6,000 Italian families lived in this Little Italy and toiled to build San Diego into the center of the world tuna industry.

With the decline of the tuna industry on the West Coast and the destruction of 35% of this Little Italy due to the construction of Interstate 5, Little Italy suffered nearly thirty years of decline. In the early 1990's, established property owners and family run business owners decided to take their fate into their own hands.

Today San Diego's Little Italy is on the brink of rebuilding. Builders and architects are building new developments and the local redevelopment agency is funding more than three million in street improvements on the main commercial corridor, India Street

"Little Italy" Albuquerque, New Mexico

As opportunities in the mining and railroad industries opened in states such as Colorado, California and New Mexico, many Italians moved westward for higher wages and the more moderate climate. Census data from 1910 shows 1,959 foreign-born Italians living in New Mexico.

While most Italian immigrants in the US were from Southern Italy, New Mexico's Italian population through 1930 was almost entirely from the North. These immigrants chose to come to New Mexico, rather than to stay with so many of their countrymen in the more industrialized Eastern and Midwestern cities, because of economic opportunity. Economic competition in New Mexico at that time was relatively non-existent.

They came to New Mexico as miners or railroaders to save money for a few years, and then enter into the business world, often to operate a saloon or a grocery store. Most Italian immigrants settled in New Mexico's urban areas but some managed farm land mainly in Central New Mexico Many Italian immigrants who had settled on the East Coast had come as skilled stone cutters and architects. These skills were in demand in New Mexico as it built up its cities and infrastructure.

Albuquerque's original Italian community settled primarily between 1st and 8th streets, around Marquette. For several generations, children of this early community tended to marry within the community and to stay as residents in this same area. Descendants of this community distinguish themselves from the large Italian population in Rio Rancho, who came from Italian communities on the East Coast, primarily New York, and who is descended from Southern Italian immigrants. Today, Albuquerque's Italian community is quite large. 2000 census data shows 25,298 people who claim Italian descent living in the area.

"Little Italy" Providence, Rode Island

In the early part of the 1900's, a wave of immigrants from Italy arrived at Providence. These immigrants settled along Spruce Street and Atwells Avenue. This was previously known as an Irish neighborhood but it was soon transformed into a densely Italian populated area. By 1905, there were 18,104 Italian-born residents living in Providence; and by 1920, 42,044. Gradually the Italian population extended into all Federal Hill (know today as "Colletto" or "Little Italy".)

Businesses at Atwells Avenue resembled the "Old Country". They were conducted on the street level spaces and the upper levels were used as residencies (much like in Italy). That area became a center of business and culture for the new Italian population.

3

The Early Service Organizations

In the early days, many Italian-Americans lived in ghettos. Other then work and family, their social activities came from the church, social clubs, and cafes. They met at each of these places on a regular basis to talk about a wide range of topics including politics, music, theater, and literature. The Italian-American immigrants gathered in two different types of cafes. The coffee houses and the café chantants or concertos. The chantants were places were musicians played a guitar or a mandolin while a singer sang as you drank your coffee and talked.

In addition to socializing at these cafes, the immigrants joined together and formed local clubs to support each other and their community. They also used these clubs to help each other in assimilating into their new environment. These clubs provided a great way of pooling their limited resources and allowing them to get things done as a group that they could not do as individuals.

Some of the early organizations, like the Order Sons of Italy, the Italian Catholic Federation, and UNICO, were all started to address the real urgent needs of the Italian immigrant to adjust to the American way of life. These organizations rose to the occasion and provided outstanding services such as teaching the immigrants how to speak English and providing them with assistance on becoming a U.S. citizen. Without them, and other organizations like them, the transition of our grandparents would have been much more difficult.

In this section, we will address a few of these early organizations and discuss how they were founded and explain their role in assisting in the assimilation of our forefathers.

Order Sons of Italy in America

Order Sons of Italy in America (OSIA) was established as a mutual aid society for the early immigrants. Today OSIA has 600,000 members and supporters and a network of more then 700 chapters coast to coast and is a leading service and advocacy organization for the nation's 25 million Italian Americans.

Originally called *"L'Ordine Figli d'Italia"*, the Sons of Italy in America was established in the Little Italy neighborhood of New York City on June 22, 1905 by Vincent Sellaro, M.D. and five other Italian immigrants who came to the United States from Italy during the great Italian migration (1880-1923).

Their goal was to create an organization for all Italian immigrants that could assist them in becoming U.S. citizens, provide health and death benefits, educational opportunities and offer assistance in assimilation in America. In the early years, OSIA established free schools to teach immigrants English and centers to help them become U.S. citizens.

The first OSIA lodges established orphanages and homes for the elderly, life insurance and mortuary funds, credit unions, welfare societies and scholarship funds to aid members in need.

In fact, my father lived in one of their orphanages for 10 years from age 6 to 16. His mother abandoned the family and him and his brothers were shipped to the orphanage. It was very hard on him but I can tell you, first hand, that the alternative was worse.

The OSIA was there for him. It allowed him to finish High School and gave him a clean home and a place to eat and sleep. He was not happy at the time. But he was very grateful to them later in his life.

My family also availed themselves of the OSIA insurance programs. Every one in the family had the life and mortuary insurance with them. They would stop by the OSIA office each week and pay the premium. It was very important in the Italian culture that you had enough money to pay for a proper burial and this organization helped you prepare for that eventual situation.

OSIA is alive and well today in a new and more expanded role.

The Italian Catholic Federation

The Italian Catholic Federation is a family oriented, non-profit fraternal organization dedicated to build family spirit and bring men and women of all ages together. The ICF slogan is "The ICF working for the Lord". The concept of a lay apostolate organization that united Italian Americans in their faith, community, and pride in their shared heritage was created by two men in San Francisco in 1924. One was Luigi Providenza and the other was Father Albert Bandini. They called the organization the Italian Catholic Federation.

Luigi Providenza was born in Genoa and was thought of as a radical idealist. He rose to the position of Chairman of Italy's Popular Party. At 26, following three attempts on his life, he immigrated to America and settled in San Francisco where he worked for a weekly Italian newspaper. In talking to Italians all over town, he found many people had lost their faith that things would get better. He wanted to help them regain their faith in the future.

Reverend Albert Bandini was the son of an influential Florentine family. He was a scholar, a poet and an attorney. He came to California at the request of the Archbishop who needed the services of Italian speaking priests. He, like Luigi, saw the depression of the Italian people and their lack of hope in a better future.

Providenza and Rev. Bandini began work in 1924 and on June 15th the first organizational meeting took place in the church of the Immaculate Conception in San Francisco's Mission District.

This awakened a "more intense Christian life among the Italian population in California". The organization, which became the Italian Catholic Federation, was envisioned to be "primarily a parochial society upon which the local pastor could rely on for his work". But it has become much more then that.

At its' peak, the organization grew to 30,000 members in 225 branches in 5 states and whose charitable work reached an uncountable number of people. For example, since 1964, the Italian Catholic Federation has awarded over $1,000,000 in scholarships to deserving students in their scholarship program. They have donated special funds for sponsoring seminarians with religious vocations; anemia research; developmentally disabled children; and organ donor awareness. They also have encouraged good citizenship through special recognition by giving annual awards for humanitarian service; Christian service; ideals of the organization; humanitarian work; and the young adult.

UNICO National, Inc.

UNICO National, Inc. is a nationwide service organization. Its membership is open exclusively to American men and women of Italian heritage. It grants scholarships awards, promotes Italian Study Chairs, observes Columbus Day with fitting programs, participates in underprivileged and handicapped children's work, charities, communities and civic activities. The organization adopted the motto, "Service above self", which has patterned the whole activity of UNICO since.

UNICO was founded in Waterbury, Connecticut in 1922 when a group of men headed by Dr. Anthony Vastola organized the first chapter to provide assistance to their community. The chapter won the good acceptance from their community and the idea spread slowly to several other cities in the East.

It was organized to provide scholarships to worthy students and give strength and force in fighting the discrimination against Italian-Americans in our Society at that time. By 1930 there were enough chapters to hold their first convention in New York. In 1947, the organization was renamed and UNICO was born. The name, translated from the Italian, means "one" or "only" or "only one of its' kind".

Since its founding, UNICO has awarded hundreds of college scholarships, raised hundreds of thousands of dollars for the establishment of Italian Study Chairs in Colleges and Universities throughout the United States, and sent thousands of children to camp. It has raised millions of dollars for local charities and in support of local drives, recognized many individuals throughout the nation for outstanding achievements and sponsored a national mental health program among its many other achievements.

Italian-American Community Services Agency.

Another early organization was the Italian-American Community Services Agency. It was founded in 1916 by leading members of the San Francisco Italian community, such as A.P. Giannini, Marco Fontana and Andrea Sbarboro to provide assimilation services to the Italian Immigrants in San Francisco. These men were successful in their own lives and wanted to help their Italian brethren.

Services include advocacy, and to promote, protect and coordinate housing, medical, nutritional and other social services for Italians and Italian-Americans in San Francisco. While many Bay Area Italians have prospered overall, there are many—particularly seniors—who rely on the Agency for service coordination even today. Today, the need is still there for older members of the Italian-American Community in North Beach who in many cases do not speak English and have lost their companions. Our immigrant forefathers taught us that we are all one big family.

All of these organizations still exist today. Three of them are national organizations that grew large by adding chapters and expanding their services from city to city.

◆   ◆   ◆

Each of these organizations needs younger members. For those of you interested in participating, they are worth a look. They do great work for the community and you get a lot out of your participation. As the Italian-American population became more integrated into the American society, the clubs change as well. Some, like the Order Sons of Italy have changed its mission for example.

Also, new clubs have emerged that are not focused on the issues of assimilation but on other issues affecting the needs of the Italian American Community such as Italian Heritage and Education and Professional Training and Career Development. Today, our cubs and organizations span a wide variety of different types addressing a wide range of different issues and purposes.

There are a number of Italian American fraternal organizations in the United States. In the remaining Chapters of this book, we will identify a number of these organizations and talk about the work that these are doing in keeping the Italian-American ideals and values alive and well in America.

We thank the founders of these early organizations for laying the foundation for the hundreds of present Italian-American organizations in the United States today.

For, as we proceed, you will see, each organization, whether it is a social, educational, professional, or heritage in nature, seems to remember it roots and continues to have a major component "to serve" as part of its mission. Most of them offer some form of scholarship, give to charity, or service their community in one way or another. It must be the Italian way!!

4

The Catholic Church: The Soul of the Community

The Catholic Church was a major contributor in the growth of the Italian-American community in the United States. It did much more than be there to provide spiritual guidance for the Italian immigrants. It was there to teach them to speak English, educate their children, and, when necessary, feed them and find them a place to live. In short, it was there to help them survive in America. I like to think of them as the soul of the Italian-American neighborhood.

From the beginning, the Italian immigrants who came to the United States during the great wave of new American immigration struggled to establish their own parishes and schools. They wanted Italian, not Irish priests to preside at daily mass, feast-day celebrations, christenings, weddings and funerals.

And ultimately they got their wish. For example, many of the Italian parishes founded in the Pennsylvania's largest cities still flourish today. For example, there are still three Italian parishes in Pittsburgh and eleven in Philadelphia today. Today Our Lady of Mt. Carmel serves many of the Catholic Italian families of Allentown, while St. Anthony's is the church of many second-and third-generation Italians who reside in Johnstown.

ROLE OF THE CATHOLIC CHURCH IN THE COMMUNITY

In the early days, the Italian immigrants saw the Catholic parishes as the center of the community and the parish school as the only source of education for their children. Italian-Americans will tell you that you cannot talk about any Italian neighborhood, without talking about the Catholic Church as the center. And, in most Italian families, the Catholic Church has been part of their family history for centuries.

In many Italian families, a brother, sister, uncle, or aunt was a member of one Catholic religious order or another. It has been part of the long-standing tradition to have at least one family member join a religious order. It was a tradition in Italy and the tradition continued as Italians immigrated to the United States.

ROLE OF THE CATHOLIC CHURCH IN ITALY

In Italy, the Catholic Church has been part of the fabric of the Italian way of life for centuries. For example, although the Italian government recognizes other religions, the Roman Catholic Church is traditionally recognized as the state church because most Italians are Roman Catholic.

All references to church records in Italy, unless otherwise noted, refer to Catholic records. In Italy, the Church has been keeping the official state records for hundreds of years on dates and places of births, marriages, and deaths. They also have detailed records on christenings and first communions. All church records were kept at the local parish church in Italy. The term parish refers to the jurisdiction of a church priest. Parishes are local congregations, usually in one town only, but sometime they include other villages in their boundaries.

The parish was so integrated into the community that, in history, the parish priest was often required to collect taxes for the state from his parishioners. He would sometimes record information about his parishioners and when he collected a tax for the state and he recorded it in a special set of volumes called the church censuses. In Latin it is called the "status animarum". This means the "state of the souls". For many years, Italy also used these records as their official census data.

Therefore it was not surprising that when the Italians moved to the new world they looked to the Catholic Church; their parishes; and their priests as an important and leading element in the community. The growth and success of my community, South Philadelphia, in my hometown of Philadelphia can be directly attributed to a number of religious people and religious institutions in the community.

However, there are a few that do stand out because of their particular importance to our Italian-American community in South Philadelphia where I wish to address in this book. They are Bishop John Neumann and organizations like the Archdiocese of Philadelphia, the Sisters of the Immaculate Heart of Mary, the Norbertines.

ARCHDIOCESE OF PHILADELPHIA & BISHOP JOHN NEUMANN

The Italian neighborhood in South Philadelphia was assisted in its' growth by the Archdiocese of Philadelphia and Bishop John Neumann primarily through the expansion of the number of its Italian-American parishes and their parish schools. This happened in the mid to late 1800s and through the early 1900s.

The Archdiocese, through able leaders like Saint John Neumann, led the way in developing a strong foundation for an excellent Catholic school system that still exist today supporting the community. It began at the end of the Civil War when Father Molyneux, the second pastor of Philadelphia, opened the first Catholic parish school in Philadelphia in 1785. It was in St. Mary's Parish.

But, it was Saint John Neumann, the fourth Bishop of Philadelphia, who made the establishment of parish elementary schools a priority in the Archdiocese and by 1860 there were seventeen parish elementary schools in Philadelphia. Although he was not Italian, Bishop Neumann was also the one that most Italians in Philadelphia remember as most caring and respecting to the Italian-American community.

The customs and the Catholic faith of the Italian immigrants were often feared by the "original' population of Philadelphia. As Catholic immigrants became more involved in 19th century America, some Evangelists believed that Catholicism was an oppressive, superstitious and aggressive religion, which would enter "their public schools". This led the Italian children to be unwelcome in the public school system of the time.

Also, the Irish were the first large group of Catholics to arrive in Philadelphia and set up Catholic Churches. The Italian immigrants were unwelcome in the then Irish churches because the Irish were trying to preserve their identity.

Bishop Neumann became Bishop of the first national parish for Italians in South Philadelphia. He was dedicated to the Italians having their own Italian church but in the interim Bishop Neumann, granted the Italians, regular use of the Cathedral Chapel for masses in their own language. At the time there were no priest to speak the Italian language and Bishop Neumann, who had studied Italian as a seminarian in Bohemia, brought them together in this chapel and talked to them in Italian.

Later, Bishop Neumann founded the first national parish for Italians in the United States. In 1852 he purchased a Methodist Church in South Philadelphia, dedicated it to St. Mary Magdalene de Pazzi, and gave them one of his seminary professors, Father John Tornatore, C.M., to be their pastor. Bishop John Neumann died on January 5, 1860 in the snow a few blocks from his new cathedral on Logan Square near his home. He was buried in a basement crypt in Saint Peter's Church, at his request, where he would be with his Redemptorist confreres.

Since the creation of the Diocese of Philadelphia in 1808, all its bishops have all been Irish. Neumann's German background made some think of him as being unsuitable to be elevated to that position. However, in his eight years as Bishop, what a difference he made. He made a special impact in the area of education. He surely silenced many of those doubters.

On arriving in Philadelphia, he learned that despite the large size and population of the diocese, no more then 500 children were attending parochial schools. Within a month of his arrival, a new Central Board of Catholic Education was created consisting of the pastor and two layman from each parish. He asked them to create a plan for the diocese and assist the parishes, particularly the poor ones, in fund raising. Results were excellent. Within a year, the number of students in parochial schools grew from 500 to 5000. After two years it was 9000.

His actions put Philadelphia in the lead in Catholic education in the United States and the South Philadelphia parishes still see the benefits of that today.

Pope Paul VI declared John Neumann a Saint in 1977 and his shrine in Philadelphia is visited by thousands each year.

◆   ◆   ◆

One of the major goals of the Catholic Church in the neighborhood was to provide a quality education to the children of the Catholic families in their parishes. This was accomplished through a number of Catholic organizations but I would like to discuss two that I am most familiar and that impacted me and were most prominent in South Philadelphia—They were the Sisters of the Immaculate Heart of Mary and the Norbertines.

SISTERS OF THE IMMACULATE HEART OF MARY

The Sisters of the Immaculate Heart of Mary is a Religious Organization of Nuns. The Immaculata Branch of the Sisters today comprises approximately 1050 Sisters who currently staff the Catholic schools in Pennsylvania, Connecticut, Virginia, Georgia, and Florida. Their origins can be traced back to 1858 when St, John Neumann, then Bishop of Philadelphia, asked Mother M. Theresa, Sister Ann and Sister M. Celestine to agree to staff St. Joseph School in Susquehanna, PA., which was formerly taught by the Holy Cross Sisters.

A second mission was quickly undertaken in Reading, PA. In a short time, applications came flooding in for the new order and the Motherhouse was transferred to West Chester, PA., near Philadelphia, in 1872. It remained there until 1966 when it moved to its present location at Immaculata, PA. Today, they teach in many of the Roman Catholic parish schools in South Philadelphia as they have from the very beginning. I attended St. Gabriel's Catholic School and I remember the Sisters of the Immaculate Heart of Jesus very well.

They were my educators throughout my early years and I owe them a lot. St. Gabriel's School was located at 29th and Dickerson Street and was part of St. Gabriel's Parish. It was founded in 1895. The boundaries of the parish were Grays ferry Avenue from the Schuylkill River to 28th Street West to Tasker Street; to 25th Street; to McKean Street. I have very fond memories of those days.

Saint Gabriel's is one of twenty-four Catholic parishes that still exist in South Philadelphia today that are all "doing God's business". They are:

South Philadelphia Roman Catholic Parishes
South of Market Street
Founded 1723-1923

Epiphany (1889)	St. Philip Neri (1840)	St. Stanislaus (1891)	St. Casimir (1893)	St Edmond (1912)
Old St. Mary's (1763)	St. Paul (1843)	St Thomas Aquinas (1885)	St. Aloysius (1894)	King of Peace (1926)
Holy Trinity (1788)	St. Mary Magdalen de Pazzi (1852)	St. Anthony's (1886)	St. Monica (1895)	St. Gabriel (1895)
St. John the Evangelist (1830)	Annunciation BVM (1860)	Sacred Heart of Jesus (1871)	Old St. Joseph's (1733)	St. Nicolas of Tolentine (1912)
St. Patrick (1839)	ST. Charles Barommeo (1868)		Our Lady of Mount Carmel (1896)	St Rita of Casia (1907)

*Years that they were founded

In fact, according to the Official Catholic Directory for 2001, there are a total of 19,008 parishes in the United States for the population of 250,000,000 people or one parish for every 13,152 people. In South Philadelphia, with 24 parishes, we have one parish for every 916 people. If you need a Catholic Church in this neighborhood, you have a choice.

Parish Segregation of Boys & Girls

In my opinion, Catholic education in the 1950's and 1960's in South Philadelphia could be defined by the term "segregation" but not in the way we think of it today i.e. not segregation between blacks and whites. It was "segregation" between boys and girls. The nuns kept us apart. For some reason, the nuns did not allow the boys and girls to socialize or even be in the same classroom. To this day, I am not sure why but I always found that it was a strange way to run a school even when I was 8 years old.

Saint Gabriel's grammar school was a Catholic Parrish school that educated both boys and girls in our neighborhood. However, the two were kept separated within the building. Each had separate classrooms; teachers; even a separate schoolyard for recess and even separate entrances into the building.

One exception to this rule was on Valentine's Day. Each February 14th, each child was permitted to bring in Valentine Cards. If you were in the 7th and 8th grade, you could actually address your card to an individual person of the opposite sex. If you were in a younger grade, you put your card in a large drum marked either boy or girl and it would be drawn out of the drum by lottery.

At the end of the day, in the usual disciplined fashion, the cards were delivered to the recipient's classroom and opened there with the appropriate cheer.

Thinking back on it, it was a very romantic way to introduce the children to the concept of Valentine day.

One thing that both boys and girls did have in common was that we were expected to dress appropriately for school. The dioceses had a dress code and all students were expected to comply. That meant a uniform was to be worn each day. The boys wore a blue blazer jacket, white shirt and tie, and dark slacks. The girls wore a school "jumper" outfit designed for the dioceses with a white blouse. While these uniforms became very boring for the kids over eight years in grammar school, it was easy on the parents since they did not have to react to style changes. In addition, there were no arguments on what you were going to wear to school each morning, it was predetermined.

The nuns did take into consideration, however, that boys and girls do, on occasion, talk to each other. The nuns were also good at demanding discipline from their students and they knew what it took to get it. There is one story that I will never forget that makes my point.

I was 13 years old in the 8th grade. The nun that taught my last period was also responsible for ringing the dismissal bell each day for the entire school. She was an older nun and each day she would go to the washroom punctually at 10 AM and 1 PM since she could not wait until dismissal at 3:30.

When she would leave for her 1:00pm bathroom break on a Friday, I jumped on the desk and turned the clock in the classroom ahead one hour in front of the laughing students. When she returned to resume class, she did not notice the change in time and when the clock turned 3:30 PM she rang the bell to dismiss us. It was not until she arrived at the Nunnery that she had learned that she had dismissed the whole school on hour early. She was furious.

The following Monday, I was found to be the culprit and I was give 6 hits of harsh lashing with an instrument called the "cat of nine tails". This is nine leather straps held together on one handle and I can attest that it does hurt.

Can you imagine a child being hit by this instrument today for such a prank? My parents had a good relationship with the Nun and thought that it served me right and that I should not have done such a thing. They were right of course but it did hurt and it gave me a great reputation in school that took me a while to live down.

Correcting My Left Hand Writing

The Nuns also had a few issues during the 1950s that I am happy to say have been resolved now. For example, I am left-handed. When I arrived for my first day of school in first grade, I tried to write with my left hand since I am left-handed.

My teacher corrected me and placed the pencil in my right hand. I am told that the thinking at the time was that writing left-handed was considered lazy and was to be corrected immediately by forcing me to write with my right hand. I spent the first two years of my schooling trying to write with my right hand. By year three, the thinking must have changed, or I wore them down, because they permitted me to use my left hand to write.

THE NORBERTINES

Another religious order that had a significant impact on South Philadelphia education was the Norbertines. In most parts of the world they are called the Canon Regular of Premontre, also know as the Premonstratensians, Norbertines, or

White Canons (in the United Kingdom).They are a group of Roman Catholic priests, brothers, and sisters whose order was founded by St. Norbert in the 12th Century at the dawn of the great reform movement of the middle ages in western Europe.

In 1995, the Order numbered 1,700 members of which 1,300 were priest and 300 were sisters. They have abbeys and missions throughout the world. In their 875 year history, they have delivered there message through living the simple life.

Why am I talking about this 12th century religious organization of European priest, brothers, and sisters here? They founded an abbey in South Philadelphia in 1934. These priests also founded the only Catholic Boys High School in South Philadelphia that I attended and graduated from in 1965: Bishop Neumann High School.

Bishop Neumann High was founded in September 1934 with the help of the Norbertines as Southeast Catholic High School for Boys. The school's name was changed to Bishop Neumann High in 1955 and Saint John Neumann High in 1978.

I also remember my high school years with the fondest of memories. Bishop Neumann High School was led by the Norbertine priests but there were priests from many other orders teaching there as well. There were also a number of lay teachers. They devoted themselves to their students in many ways. Naturally, I believe I received a great education and it allowed me the opportunities that I have received throughout my life. But, in addition, the priests were also there when you needed them as counselors and friends. Growing up in such a poor neighborhood with so many competing forces, it brought you into many con-flicts during my four years in high school. They were always there for me. And there were the fun times too.

The school was run very strictly and by the "rules". I have lost count on the number of detentions that I received for going the wrong way on the staircases. The staircases were marked "up" and 'down" to control the flow of student traffic between classes. I would use the wrong one to 'take a shortcut" when I was late for class. I would usually get caught by a teacher but I always seemed to do it again anyway. A detention was spending time after school in a dark room for a two-hour period supervised by a very strict teacher.

The High School Dances

As I mentioned earlier, the boys and girls were kept separated throughout the day and in most of other recreational activities. These dances were one of the few exceptions to this rule. This was an organized Catholic activity were boys and girls could get together. But these dances were well regulated and well supervised and, by today's standards, the teenager's would be appalled by how controlling they were.

Bishop Neumann High School held a dance every Saturday night. "Everybody who was anybody attended". It was the place to be on Saturday if you were between 15 and 18 years old and you were Catholic from South Philadelphia.

First, there was a very strict dress code and the Bishop Neumann High School's Disciplinarian (a priest) was at the front door of the gymnasium to enforce the dress code for men and women alike. Next, the chaperones (usually priests and nuns) were roaming throughout the gym enforcing the manner of dancing as well as the closeness. Imagine dancing with your girlfriend with nuns and priest roaming throughout the gym.

If you left the building before the dance was over, your parents would get a letter from a priest telling them what time you left and with whom. Now that I look back on them, I can see how well planned they really were.

St. Marie Goretti High School

The St. Marie Goretti Catholic High School for Girls was established in South Philadelphia under the direction of John Cardinal O'Hara on September 7, 1955. Reverend Francis X. Tracey, a professor at the St. Thomas Moore High School was the first principal together with thirty-four members of seven religious communities. Priests ran the school until June of 1986 when Sister Teresa Mary, RSM former principal of Bishop Conwell High School in Levittown, Pennsylvania became the first woman principal.

The girls were required to wear uniforms during schools hours, as were all other Catholic students in the Diocese. There uniforms included a blue dress with the school insignia and a belt. The hem was required to be at least three inches below the knee. It was very unfashionable in those days and the girls hated the uniform and were embarrassed to be seen in such an out-of date dress.

It was a funny site to see the parade of girls as they left the school building each day hiking their dresses under their belt so that their hemline would be above their knee rather then below their knee. This way they would be somewhat in fashion as they met their boyfriends or groups before going home for dinner.

There was also an incident that happened at St. Maria Goretti's in 2003. Apparently, according to newspaper reports, about 20 Catholic school girls from the school chased down a man who had been flashing at them near their high school. The girls tackled him to the ground and held him there until police arrived. It is nice to know that the St. Maria Goretti teachers are still educating aggressive, take-charge, young women who join together to protect their interest and that of their neighborhood.

Both schools remained independent until 2004 when, Anthony Cardinal Bevilacqua accepted the recommendation from the Secretary of Catholic Education in the Philadelphia Archdiocese to consolidate Saint John Neumann High School and Saint Marie Goretti High School. The reason was decreased enrollments at both schools. The Cardinal stated, however, "I trust that the consolidation will create a stronger Catholic high school for the future". I hope his words prove true.

My wife Phyllis in her high school uniform in 1965

Now that I look back on it, it was quite obvious that the priest and nuns in our Parish and in the High Schools acted as an extension of our parents. They played a vital and ongoing role in raising the Italian American children in the community. They participated in the ongoing rearing, correcting, and financial support of the children from first grade through High School and did a very effective job.

PART II

The Traditions, Values & Superstitions

5

My Neighborhood: South Philadelphia

Many readers will think of Philadelphia as one of the most ethnically diverse Cities on the east coast and that it is the fifth largest city in the country. Historians will remember Philadelphia as the city that was founded by the Indians as Shackamaxon on the Lenape River (later named the Delaware). They will remember it as the city that William Penn later received a land grant from King Charles II of England in March 1681 to rename Philadelphia. The city's whose name mean's "city of brotherly love" in ancient Greek.

Penn founded the city on two basic principals: *freedom for every man and religious tolerance.* These two principals seem very profound today because as you will see in reading this book, they have been practiced in the lives of many of the everyday people in South Philadelphia for over 300 years. It was also the stage for many history-making events including its role in the American Revolution; the signing of the Declaration of Independence; the Center of the Independence Movement; The creation of the American Flag; Founding of Electricity; The Liberty Bell; and many more.

Many famous citizens lived and worked in Philadelphia including Thomas Jefferson; Ben Franklin; Marion Anderson; Mario Lanza; John Barrymore; Wilt Chamberlain; Bill Cosby; and Grace Kelly.

Granny, Aunt Roz, Cousin Julia, Cousin Danny, My Wife Phyllis, & Her
Mom Mary on Sigel Street in South Philadelphia in 1948

But to me, I still think of Philadelphia as my home and the place where I was raised. And when I think of my home, I think of South Philadelphia—the neighborhood where I lived for many years and the home of the Italian-American community in Philadelphia.

During the first 100 years, the population of Philadelphia grew very fast as settlers from Ireland, England, Germany, Italy and many other parts of Europe came to Philadelphia. For example, on October 6, 1683, thirteen Quaker families from the German state of Krefeld arrived in Philadelphia. From the beginning, they lived on the northern outskirts of Philadelphia in their settlement called Germantown.

By the first American census in 1790, this little settlement had grown and Pennsylvania's German population reached 225,000, which was one third of the entire state's population at the time. Over time, Germans bakers' tool and die makers, and other craftsman crowded the North Philadelphia neighborhoods.

Also, between 1820 and the Civil War (1861-1865), over 80,000 Irish migrated to Philadelphia and settled throughout the city. Immigrants from Poland moved to the industrial sections of the city like Richmond and Manayunk.

In the eighteenth century on, Philadelphia received a small number of professional artists from Italy. These artists were too small in number to establish much of a presence in Philadelphia, but they did contribute to the City's knowledge of the Italian art. In the nineteenth century came craftsmen from Italian regions as primarily temporary migration workers for economic survival since times were very bad in Italy. After the American Civil War, these migrants began to remain and bring their families. Their numbers increased with the late nineteenth century building boom and the mass Italian migration.

As with the rest of the country, mass migration of peasant families from Southern Italy began in Philadelphia in the 1880's and lasted through the 1920's. These immigrants were new to the big cities and to industrialization. They found jobs as unskilled labor in the construction and garment industries. Their presence grew in the city and created a demand for Italian goods, services, and institutions.

The Italian immigrants brought different kinds of culture and tradition to Philadelphia based on their background in Italy. Some brought regional and folk traditions, while others brought family-based crafts, special gender-based skills, and knowledge of the national culture of the Italian elite.

The Italian laborers who came to Philadelphia in the 1870s usually arrived in New York City and traveled to Philadelphia by rail. Many were hired to lay track by the Pennsylvania and the Reading Railroads. Italian immigration to Philadelphia was still primarily from the provinces of southern Italy with steamship passenger service to Philadelphia beginning in 1908, a number of Italian families traveled directly to Philadelphia. Italian immigrants found work as makers of wearing apparel, women's shoes and Stetson hats. They also were carpenters in the cabinet shop of Victor/RCA and worked on municipal public-works projects. Later they jumped to more skilled jobs like masons, bricklayers, plumbers and electricians. This provided the immigrant families with a degree of economic security and enabled them to assist other family members and former villagers in finding employment. In addition, this work also enabled Philadelphia's Italians to save some of their wages and purchase homes in South and West Philadelphia.

The Italian immigrants of Philadelphia formed hundreds of clubs, organizations both to help their countrymen adjust to life in the United States and to preserve their language and cultural heritage. In May 1904, a number of Italian-

American Philadelphians organized the Italian Federation of Societies to coordinate the Italian community's mutual aid efforts. By 1930, the Federation had thirty-one member societies. One social organization that was important was the Order of Brotherly Love, founded in 1925. The Order established camps in various sections of the city and aided impoverished children and widows.

While Philadelphia and Pittsburgh attracted most of the Italians who came to Pennsylvania, the Commonwealth's smaller cities, such as Reading, Scranton, Easton, and Bethlehem, also acquired Italian neighborhoods as well.

Wherever in Northeast they settled, the Italians faced many hardships. Many Italian immigrants worked in jobs that were low paying and hazardous. Many worked in the steel and coal industries. This prompted them to support the labor unions. However, Italian workers took part in the day-to-day struggles to organize those trades and industries in which they predominated, such as stonecutting, garment making and barbering.

In all three of these trades, the same pattern of organization was followed. First, groups of Italian workers formed a mutual aid society. These Italian community organizations, such as Philadelphia's Italian Tailors' Society, which formed in 1884, and Stella d'Italia, an association of barbers which was formed in 1886, provided insurance and death benefits for their members. These mutual aid societies paved the way for later unions that received support both within and outside the Italian community.

In the early 20th century, Pennsylvania Italians were active in unions, among them the Granite Cutters' International Association, the Stonemasons' International Union of America, the Journeymen Tailors' International Union of America, and the Journeymen Barbers' International Union of America.

Many Italian immigrants could not find or afford decent housing. Some had to take their children out of school to secure jobs to contribute to the family income.

Like members of other ethnic groups in Pennsylvania, the descendants of Italian immigrants have moved into all levels and activities of society, nationally as well as in the Commonwealth. They became prominent in the arts, law, science, government, commerce, manufacturing and finance. A number stand out for leading the way from newly arrived immigrant to distinguished citizen. Some Philadelphians that stand out are discussed below.

The first Italians to arrive in Philadelphia in the mid-eighteenth century established a new community and one of the first "Little Italies" in South Philadelphia. The Italians found Philadelphia attractive because the city was the cultural, economic, and political center of North America in the early 19th century. They generally received a warm welcome because of the high regard the Americans had for the Italian culture.

In the Philadelphia area, they first started working in the coal mines of Scranton, PA and Wilkes-Barre, PA and in the quarries of Roseto, PA. They also worked in the fruit orchards of South Jersey and in urban Philadelphia. By the late 19th century the city contained a large Italian population in South Philadelphia.

Between 1880 and 1920 the number of Italians grew into vibrant Italian communities of Calabresi, Abruzzesi, Siciliani, and Pugiesi in the Delaware Valley. Despite the poor economic conditions that they found themselves in they were emotionally bound to each other and called themselves *"paesani"* (friends). They were bound together though their traditions, superstitions, ceremonies and language and with the hopes of a bright future in this new and promising land.

Three famous early South Philadelphians included Charles Baldi, Walter Alessandroni, and Mario Lanza.

Charles C.A. Baldi (1862–1930) was born in the province of Salerno and came to Philadelphia in 1876. After working in the mining industry in Pottsville, he and his brothers started a coal business. Later Baldi started a real estate and banking business and was a mortician. He was active in the publication of L'Opinione, an Italian-language newspaper, and he supported many Italian-American clubs and associations. Baldi was involved in politics and in efforts to improve public education.

Walter E. Alessandroni (1912–1966) was born in Philadelphia, the son of Italian immigrants. He was a graduate of Villanova University and the University of Pennsylvania's School of Law. Alessandroni career was as an attorney, Governor William W. Scranton appointed him attorney general of Pennsylvania. At the time of his death, he was considered a prospective candidate for lieutenant governor.

The famous tenor, Mario Lanza (1921–1959), was christened Alfredo Arnold Corozza in South Philadelphia in 1921. His stage surname was his mother's maiden name. During World War II, he sang in the U.S. Army's Special Services, appearing in "On the Beam" and "Winged Victory."

After the war, he gave concerts and became a top recording artist. He signed with the MGM motion picture studio in 1947. Among his films were "That Midnight Kiss," 1949; "The Toast of New Orleans," 1950; "The Great Caruso," 1951; "Because you're Mine," 1952; "Student Prince," 1954; "Serenade," 1956; and "Seven Hills of Rome," 1958. Lanza died in October, 1959. His death was mourned by the thousands whose lives he had touched through music.

Mario's Father, Antonio Cocozza was a World War I hero and had a fine collection of grand opera records. At age of 5 "Freddy" showed a great interest in the family Victrola which regularly played recording of Caruso and he would sing along with Caruso's records. He knew he wanted to become a singer at an early age. Mario died of a massive heart attach on October 7, 1959.

During the period from 1910 to 1914, at the height of the immigration from southern and eastern Europe, Philadelphia was the third most important immigrant port in the country. The First World War put an end to that growth and by 1923 only one ship, the old *Haverford*, carried immigrants to Philadelphia.

At the turn of the century, Philadelphia led the nation in such diverse industries as production of locomotives, streetcars, saws, hosiery, hats, leather, goods, and cigars, while it ranked second in the manufacture of drugs and chemicals and in the refining of sugar and petroleum. Because most of these industries required only skilled labor and semi-skilled workers, Philadelphia attracted very few Slavic immigrants. Those immigrants were more attracted to cities such as Pittsburgh, Detroit, and Chicago.

Philadelphia is a city of neighborhoods. According to the Philadelphia NIS neighborhood data Base, there are sixty-nine recognized neighborhoods in Philadelphia. For a neighborhood with such a small population (22,300 people in a city of 1.5 million in 2000) South Philadelphia had many famous people who lived there including Thomas Jefferson in 1793, Marion Anderson, Mario Lanza, Frankie Avalon, Mayor Frank Rizzo, Chubby Checker, Temple University's coach John Chaney, and Larry Fine of the Three Stooge's comedy act.

In addition to South Philadelphia, other significant neighborhoods include Center City, Chestnut Hill, Cobbs Creek, Fairmount, Frankford, Germantown, Girard Estates, Grays Ferry, and Mayfair. Each of these has their own distinct flair and distinction and you would notice that there are differences just by visiting them and walking around their main gathering areas. According to Philadelphia records, South Philadelphia is also the oldest neighborhood in the city at over 300 years old.

There are some other key points you should keep in mind. Like many Italian-American communities in the United States, it is a residential community. Its buildings are over 92% residentially compared to 80% within the city as a whole. The residential properties are heavily owner occupied (69.5% vs. 59.3% for the city as a whole) and the city has a very low number of multi-family properties (0.51% vs. 3.09% for the city as a whole.

South Philadelphia is framed by South Street on the north and the Delaware and Schuykill Rivers on the east and west. Many of the residents of South Philadelphia live in what is know as residential row homes (92.6% compared to 63.5% in Philadelphia as a whole).

Some of the key statistics related to present day South Philadelphia according to this database are:

South Philadelphia
Summary Data

Description	Year	South Philadelphia	Philadelphia
Population	2000	22,000	1,517,550
Res. Properties %	2004	92.6%	80.9%
Multi-Fam Prop%	2004	0.51%	3.09%

Res. Row Houses	2004	92.6%	63.5%
Res. Sales Price	2002	$45,000	$55,000
Res. Sales Price Change %	2001-2002	18.08%	14.58%
Children Under 18	2000	23.88%	25.27%
Owner Occupied	2000	69.49%	59.25%

As I stated, many of the residents live in row houses. This "row house" tradition dates back to the time of William Penn in 1682 when he laid out the "greene country towne" rows of buildings sharing sidewalls with neighbors were the main form of urban housing in the 1800s. These were tight-knit developments that stood shoulder to shoulder.

This "row house" form of building was very compact and it was very convenient for people to walk around the entire community. It also was variable enough to accommodate a broad spectrum of economic classes. If you were rich, you could have high ceilings, three-story town houses built along main streets or overlooking parks. If you were poor, like many people in South Philadelphia, you lived in tiny row homes, lower ceilings, with two stories, built along alleys or behind larger houses.

The homes are very close together and usually are intermingled with stores and restaurants and other small retail establishments. Many of the homes were built in the late 1800s and early 1900s with some "newer' homes built in the mid 1900s. These newer homes were built in the south and west sections of the area. There was also a federally funded housing project built in the west for the very low income housing need in the area.

Because Philadelphia workers were well paid they could afford the row homes built between 1880 and 1920. By 1920, nearly half of all Philadelphians own their own residences. As in Italy, the South Philadelphia Italian mother was the central figure and all social activities evolved around the family, social functions, and the church.

The Italian community grew up around Christian Street. Today this area is known as Bella Vista and is said to be oldest Italian neighborhood in the city. Its street boundaries are South Street to Washington Avenue, west side of Sixth Street to 11ᵗʰ Street. The name is Italian and means "pretty view." Many Italian immigrants who entered Philadelphia via Washington Avenue gravitated to the neighborhood. Early settlers were natives of Spadafora, Sicily.

The locally famous Palumbo Restaurant was located in this neighborhood and the family's boarding home for immigrants was built here as well. The first Italian immigrant bathhouse later became the Fante-Leone Pool at Montrose and Darien streets. Also, as mentioned, Alfred "Freddie" Cocozza, better known as opera legend Mario Lanza, was born here and made his first public appearance here. He sang the Ave Maria at St. Mary Magdalene de Pazzi Church where he also served as an altar boy.

Although they recognized class distinctions among themselves, Italians speaking a common language could fraternize in this "Little Italy" as an independent world in Philadelphia. The social life historically revolved around weddings, christenings, street processions in honor of patron saints, and outing where "stornelli" would play from mandolins and bocce would be played.

In other occasions, meals would bring people together. Someone would prepare a favorite pasta dish with tomato sauce ("*gravy*" in Philadelphia) and people would get together and eat and tell stories and enjoy themselves.

But it would be a mistake to think that the Italian community in South Philadelphia was of one mind in the early days. There were two very distinct groups of South Philadelphia at that time. One group came from northern Italy and was of northern prominenti. These were the artisans and merchants who befriended American notables of the time and founded many of the significant South Philadelphia Institutions, including St. Mary Magdalene de Pazzi and the Societa di Unione e Fratellanza Italiana. Another group was the working-class who came from the southern part of Italy and Sicily. As you would expect, they had very little but their pride and their families

This growth in the Italian community led to a growing market for imported products (coffee; olive oil; salami etc.) and the expansion of business opportunities for grocery store owners and importers in the community. V. D' Ambrosio

Company at Eight & Fitzwater and C.C.A. Baldi and Brothers on South Eight Street both opened to meet these needs.

South Philadelphia came to be known as the Little Italy of the Philadelphia, with Ninth Street as the focal point of so many quality shops and stores. There were a number of grocery stores with hand-roped cheeses hanging from the ceiling, black waxed cheese wheels, barrels of pickles and olives, crates of dried fish. There was a mixture of fragrant and sharp aromas. There were wooden stalls of imported coffee, herbs, shelves of imported extra virgin olive oil, tomato paste, home made pasta (pappardelle cutter for noodles). The sawdust on the floor gave it the final touch

Much of Ninth Street is still unchanged. However there were some features that have disappeared, like the indoor push-cart market. Local Louise Simpson has led a tour of Ninth Street called "Chef's Tour of the Italian Market" for a number of years. She also is the author of the book called Italian Food and Folklore. She has shopped there a long time and went to the market almost every day for many years.

She acknowledges that vegetarian staples such as tofu or tempeh aren't available at the Market. She also says that vendors may display dried beans or grains next to globs of fatback. She says that low-fat cheeses are scarce and that "low-fat mozzarella would taste like glue". Some of her tips for shopping on Ninth Street include: Don't bring your pet. Don't fondle the produce; instead, do ask growers to cut into produce for your inspection and compare prices at each stand before buying, but don't badger a grower for lower prices

An Italian language newspaper was also printed early in the 1900s in South Philadelphia. "L'Opinione" announced births, deaths, and marriages as well as other news and entertainment, and the latest news from Italy.

Some of Our Friends in the Neighborhood took time out for a Picture in 1953

<u>Religious Separation</u>

When I was growing up in South Philadelphia in the 1950s and 1960s, it was a racially mixed neighborhood with a wide variety of nationality represented including Irish, Germans, Blacks, Pols, and others. However, the Italians were so dominant in the neighborhood that it clearly earned the name "Little Italy" in Philadelphia.

As most good Italian-American's, when I was old enough, I registered at my parish school, St Gabriel's at 30th and Dickerson Streets. In my neighborhood, it was a long commute because it was about a mile walk. Most children lived much closer to their schools. When I was growing up, I also felt a form of religious separation everyone. It seemed that everyone that I knew was Catholic and attended a Catholic school. There was a public school only one city block from my home but I was in my school before the students arrived there and I came home from school after the children left. I never remember really seeing anyone go in or out of that building.

Our neighborhood was mostly inhabited by second generation Italians. That is, their parents emigrated from Italy. Since Italy is so predominantly Catholic, it seemed like everyone I knew was Catholic. I am sure that there were a lot of students that went to the public school but I never met them. This led to a lack of understanding and to a potential lack of distrust. As we grew older our first introduction to the public school children was through sports.

I remember my first experience was playing a football game with a public middle school (grades 6-8). As usual, the Nuns came to all of our football games. They stayed on the side lines and I do believe that they said payers for us to win at each game. But I think their payer machine was especially working hard for this game since this was a non-Catholic team we were playing. The payers worked too. We won. But I do remember that I twisted a knee.

__It was a Dangerous Neighborhood Also__

Despite the efforts of the family and the community, the neighborhood still had its bad elements. There were organized crime, gangs, other types of crime, and other problems that had to be addressed when raising children. One such story that comes to mind that impacted me happened in the summer of 1961.

It was an August night. The night was very calm and the sky was very clear. Every night since we broke for summer vacation we spent the night on the Street corner at 28th & Tasker. I was a 10th grader at Bishop Neumann High School. I was "hanging out" on a street corner like many kids in South Philadelphia in those days on a warm night in August 1961.

I was there with five of my friends from school. All of us were about the same age. We were telling stories about our day and making jokes about our school. Suddenly, the silence of the night was broken. There was a burst of screams and a gang of boys ran down the street with their one hand waving knives and their other hand holding bats.

We had no weapons and had no idea why this attack was taking place. We knew the attackers were the gang who hung on the street corner at 31st & Morris but we had no idea why they would attack us and what they thought we did to them. In minutes it was over. I, and a number of my friends, had been stabbed and beaten.

The attack ended as quickly as it began. It was a warning that the neighborhood was changing. 31st & Morris was now gang territory and we were being warned that we were not welcomed. It is a hard lesson for people who have grown up in a neighborhood where there are no barriers.

Neighborhood Vendors

Another fond memory about the neighborhood was the parade of street vendors. During the course of a lazy Saturday afternoon there came a parade of vendors. It began with the Watermelon Man in his long wagon leaded with watermelons. He'd shout at the top of his lungs at 6am waking up the entire neighborhood. Pretty soon there followed the vegetable man, also with a horse-drawn wagon.

Next the filthy junk man slowly made his way up the block. There was also a knife-sharpening truck and the Good Humor Man. There were also amusement rides like the whip and pony rides. The streets had a lot of activity all day.

My Wife Phyllis on a Vendor's Pony on a South Philadelphia Street in 1951

Cigarette Venders

As I mentioned, there were some vendors that were selling illegal products in the neighborhood as well. Our parents were continually trying to make sure that we did not get involved with the wrong crowd and "lose our moral compass". One way that it was done easily in the neighborhood in those days was to sell stolen cigarettes or cigarettes that were smuggled into the state without paying the appropriate taxes.

There were a number of smokers in Philadelphia then, especially in South Philadelphia, where smoking was such a part of Italian-American way of life. Cigarette consumption was not measured in cigarettes or packs but by cartons. The high tobacco taxes and because it appeared that South Philadelphia authorities tolerated street vendors hawking contraband cigarettes led to the existence of this practice for a number of years while I was growing up.

Vendors would recruit young Italian-American boys to sell these cigarettes on the street and give them a percentage of the sales. It would be a bad way to start out your business career by doing so an immoral act and breaking the law. But it was one of the pitfalls of living in the neighborhood so you had to be careful. It was a way of making a fast buck but starting your life on the wrong track.

6

Italian Holiday Traditions

The holidays were a special time in South Philadelphia. Everyone in the neighborhood worked very hard throughout the year and when the holidays came around it was time to be with family and friends and enjoy each other's company. It was also time to remember previous fun times and to celebrate old traditions. In this Chapter, I will describe some of the Italian family traditions that I remember from my days in the neighborhood. We will first discuss Holiday traditions.

Christmas Traditions

Christmas was very different when I was a young boy from what it is today. For example, it was not as commercialized and it was very centered on family and traditions.

In my early childhood, I didn't make lists of toys that I wanted like my children did when they were young. Instead, I wrote letters to my mother and father expressing how much I loved them and the family. Traditionally, these letters were read after dinner on Christmas Eve. I received some gifts but the letter was intended to remind me of the primary purpose for the Holiday.

One tradition you often hear of in the United States is "if you are not good, you will get coal in your stocking". Well, this actually stems from the tradition of La Befana. The story is told that on the night that Jesus was born, the three Wise Men had stopped by this woman's house to ask for directions. Afterward they had asked her to join them, but she refused.

La Befana is one of Italy's oldest and most celebrated legends. Each year on January 6 the children of Italy awaken in hopes that La Befana has made a visit to their house. Over the years the Epiphany has been a more celebrated holiday for the children of Italy than even Christmas.

As legend has it the three Wise Men were in search of the Christ child when they decided to stop at a small house to ask for directions. Upon knocking, an old woman holding a broom opened the door slightly to see who was there. Standing at her doorstep were three colorfully dressed men who were in need of directions to find the Christ child. The old woman was unaware of who these three men were looking for and could not point them in the right direction.

Prior to the three men leaving, they kindly asked the old woman to join them on their journey. She declined because she had much housework to do. After they left she felt as though she had made a mistake and decided to go and catch up with the kind men. After many hours of searching she could not find them. Thinking of the opportunity she had missed the old woman stopped every child to give them a small treat in hopes that one was the Christ child. Each year on the eve of the Epiphany she sets out looking for the baby Jesus. She stops at each child's house to leave those who were good treats in their stockings and those who were bad a lump of coal.

Later on, a shepherd stopped by to ask her for directions as well, and then also asked her to join him to come pay respects to the baby Jesus, but she refused again. Later that night, she saw a great bright star in the sky and then reconsidered going to look for the stable where Jesus was. She had collected some toys for her own child that had died, to give to the baby Jesus. But, she could not find the stable. So to this day, she goes around looking for Jesus and leaves toys for the good children and coal for the bad ones.

Throughout my life, my mother and my wife will not take down the Christmas decorations, nor will the holidays end, until January 6, the Feast of the Epiphany when the season of Christmas has officially ended.

Some of the fine Italian traditions are still in place today. It's not all about one day, but in fact from Christmas Eve (the real day of celebration, not Christmas Day), all the way to the Epiphany in January.

My wife Phyllis with her family Christmas Tree on Christmas Day

<u>Nativity Scene</u>

When my wife Phyllis was young, her grandmother began purchasing large pieces to one of the biggest nativity scenes I have ever seen.

These are the scenes about the birth of Christ in the Gospels of St. Luke and St. Matthew. It tells us about the manger, the shepherds and the three Wise Men. These sites give us a chance to see what it was like the day that Christ was born. You would expect this scene would be displayed in a town square but, each year, she displayed it proudly in the small living room in her small row home in South Philadelphia.

One of my fondest memories as a child was to take a ride and view the beautiful nativity scenes that were erected throughout the neighborhood each Christmas. The popularity of these large statues, they are called *presepi* in Italy, started in Italy in the 17th century when it was fashionable to find them in palaces and homes of wealthy citizens. The new found enthusiasm of erecting a *presepi* during

Christmas may be contributed to Saint Gaetano who openly encouraged people to create the *presepi* as a sign of devotion. It wasn't until the later part of the 19th century that these *presepi* became apart of family traditions in nearly every home in Italy.

This set is a beautiful piece of art and is a prized possession of the families that own them. I know that Phyllis' grandmother cherished her *presepi* until the day she died and the family still think fondly of their grandmother every time they see it at Christmas time.

Another Christmas Eve tradition, that serves as an alternative to Christmas Eve Mass (mass would then be attended the next morning), is the tradition of the Italian nativity scene, or Crib, and procession in the family home. In some South Philadelphia homes where nativity scenes are created by families they perform a ritual. People travel from one church to another looking at the beautiful scenes. The Crib traditionally consists of figurines made of papier mache or ceramic. Mary, Joseph, and the baby Jesus were joined by an ox and a donkey that warmed the infant with their breath

Just before midnight, the youngest person in the family would lead the procession to the family nativity scene in the house. Traditional carols were sung, and each person carried a lighted candle. At midnight, the candles are extinguished, and the figurine of the infant was nested in the manger. This signified the birth of the Christ Child. The procession passed the manger, each person stopped to kiss the infant's cheek.

Granny's Nativity Scene in her small row home in South Philadelphia
(1950)

Christmas Eve Fish Dinner

Many Italians celebrate Christmas Eve with the traditional Seven Fish Dinner. It is a custom that goes back for centuries. Not every Italian celebrates the tradition of a formal Christmas Eve Fish Dinner. During most of my life, my family was very poor, so they just ate tuna fish mixed in with macaroni and that was our Christmas Eve dinner. My wife laughs when I tell her my tuna fish story but it is the truth. However, in those years when we could afford a tradition feast, it was a great treat.

But, no matter what you had for dinner, it is a tradition that no meat is eaten on Christmas Eve in recognition of the upcoming birth of the baby Jesus. Instead, dinner is usually a seven-fish meal comprised of an elaborate spread that can include cold shellfish cocktails and hot fish dishes, as well as the roasted peppers and antipasti.

The origins of this feast vary depending on who you ask and how long you have for the response. Naturally traditions have changed, but many have kept this tradition, and as midnight brings Christmas day mom would start cooking the sausage for Christmas Dinner. We would often be eating would until the late/ early morning hours. The traditional is to serve seven fishes at the meal. Some say it is because it took God 7 days to create the universe others say it is because there are seven sacraments.

The tradition at my wife's house, and almost all the other Italian-American homes in South Philadelphia, was to have a 7 fish dinner on Christmas Eve. Some think that it is perhaps one representing each day of the week, but most traditions come from the observance of the Cena della Vigilia, the wait for the miraculous birth of Christ in which early Christians Catholics fasted on Christmas Eve until after receiving communion at Midnight Mass.

In later years it became a penitential day, meaning that all foods except meat were allowed. Other theories include: three fish representing the three Wise men; three representing the Holy Trinity and one representing Jesus and others go as high as serving thirteen fish representing Jesus and the 12 apostles. After midnight, meat dishes, such as pasta and meatballs, are offered. Pork and turkey are also favorites of this post-midnight feast. Christmas dinner is also accompanied by a number of traditional sweets, such as panettone, which is a kind of Italian fruit cake, and is a traditional gift given upon visiting family and friends.

Panettone can be purchased at a number of stores in South Philadelphia. It can also be made from scratch. Other Christmas sweets also include torrone, a kind of nougat, and panforte, which is a thick honey candy made with hazelnuts, ginger and almonds, and which is also served at Easter. All Christmas sweets contain nuts. Nuts were a symbol of fertility, and the consumption of them was thought to help to increase the size and health of flock and family. Honey is also frequently used in these desserts as an offering to insure the sweetness of the New Year.

Christmas Eve Fish Dinner at wife Phyllis's parent's House in 1950.
Around the table was Aunt Phyllis, Uncle Mike, Great Uncle Joe, Granny,
Phyllis & Tony. Mom was in the Kitchen.

New Year's Day

New Year's was a time of reawakening and renewal in the neighborhood. It was an Italian tradition to eat lentils on New Year to gain fortune and happiness in the coming year. On New Year's Day, our family would eat "cotechino con lenticchie" which is a dish consisting of pork sausage served on a bed of lentils. My father told me the story that eating "lenticchie" as the first meal of the New Year will bring you good luck.

Our neighbors followed the Italian tradition of throwing their old china dishes out the window at midnight. It symbolizes renewal and replenishment. My mother would tell me that they just wanted their husband to buy them new dishes.

One of the traditions that my friend's mother would do each year is collect new coins such as a pennies, nickels, dimes, quarters, half dollars and dollar coins. She would place them facing up and put them on the window sill before midnight on New Year's Eve to bring good luck as we pass from the old year to the new. Our neighbors always played the game of tombola, an Italian version of bingo, on New Year's Eve. Many Italians in the neighborhood reserved the game for Christmas Eve while they are waiting to go to midnight Mass.

St. Valentine's Day

Many South Philadelphia couples became engaged on Valentine's Day, February 14. The shops would sell traditional china baskets and cups filled with Valentine candies and tied with ribbon which you gave as Valentine presents. Is it not strange that Saint Valentine, who was know for his chastity, became the patron saint of lovers? Here is the history behind it.

In Roman times, Emperor Claudius II decreed marriage forbidden for soldiers. A priest named Valentine ignored this decree and encouraged young people to marry. For this, he was sentenced to prison and executed on February 14th.

Also another story is: There is also an old English belief that birds choose their mates on February 14. In any case, the Valentine's Day we know today probably derived from a combination of many legends. Some traced the origins of Valentine's Day to the ancient Roman festival called Lupercalia. The festival of Lupercalia on February 15 was to ensure protection from wolves. During the celebration, young men whipped people with strips of animal hide. Women took the blows because they believed it made them more fertile.

After the Romans conquered Britain in the year 43 AD, the British borrowed many of these Roman festivals. Writers link the festival of Lupercalia with Valentine's Day because of the similar date and the connection with fertility.

Many Italian-Americans were engaged on February 14th. I guess it is convenient for Italian men remembering the date of your engagement as the years go by.

Carnivale

Another holiday celebrated in our neighborhood was Carnivale. Carnivale is the period preceding Lent, which begins on Ash Wednesday. The name Carnivale is derived from the Lenten practice of giving up meat. It refers to the time of preparation just before the Lenten abstinence. This celebration is also related to the winter celebration of Saturnalia, when people were permitted to do almost anything they pleased.

In our neighborhood, a Carnivale celebration included Italian food and music and the wearing of masks and costumes was a tradition for many years.

Easter Sunday

Pasqua or Easter Sunday was a very sacred season that was celebrated with many special Italian customs and traditions. It was an important religious holiday and an important family celebration where Italian customs and traditions added so much to the beautiful celebration. It began with Easter Sunday mass with everyone dressed in his or her best dresses, bonnets, suits and ties. We went to mass at the church, visited our deceased relatives at the cemetery and had a traditional day-long banquet.

Brings salvation and the resurrection of Jesus Christ as Christians celebrate the foundation of their faith. One of the highlights of the banquet was dessert. It our house the dessert on Easter was usually the Fiadone. The Fiadone was a special Easter-only treat that was made in the neighborhood but each family seemed to have a slight variation on the theme and my wife's grandmother seemed to have the tastiest.

My research indicates that there are a variety of definitions of what a Fiadone is depending on what region of Italy you come from and what family recipe you have. It can be anything from a cheesecake to a cheese pie. Our family Fiadone is the equivalent of a cheese torte. It is neither a cheesecake nor a cheese pie but somewhere in between the two. In the traditional Italian style it is only slightly sweet. It is, however, very rich, and should be served in thin slices. Only the finest fresh whole milk ricotta should be used in this recipe.

7

Other Traditions & Memories

There are so many other Italian-American traditions that I could write volumes on this subject alone. However, for this book, I will concentrate on the few traditions that are most vivid in my memory. They include the Italian traditions of Naming of Children; Italian Street Painting; First Communion Dresses, and the South Philadelphia art of "Window Dressing". Other memories that we will discuss in this chapter will be the famous dance The Tarantella; Tarot cards; Limoncello and games such as stickball.

Naming Children

Have you ever wondered why there are so many Marias and Tonys in each Italian family? One reason is that in my neighborhood like in many Italian-American neighborhoods, many of the Italian-Americans named their children according to the Italian Tradition.

Since at least the sixteenth century, tradition has dictated how Italian parents name their children. My grandfather told me that it was important that you followed this tradition. In fact, it was considered an insult if you did not. You were going against you heritage. You were insulting your family. A couple's first son is given the name of the father's father; the first daughter is given the name of the father's mother. The second son is given the name of the mother's father; the second daughter is given the name of the mother's mother.

Subsequent children are given their parents' names, or the names of favorite or unmarried or deceased aunts and uncles. Because of this custom, the same given names reappear in Italian family's generation after generation. Knowing the birth order of siblings, therefore, often provides a clue to the names of their grandparents. However, exceptions do occur. For example, a grandfather might suggest that the grandson be baptized instead with the name of a son of his who died in infancy many years earlier. This is common when no other member of the family bears the name of that deceased infant.

Such a wish would be honored, and a subsequent grandson would be given this grandfather's name. Or a grandmother may ask that the granddaughter be named for a saint to whom she holds a special devotion. In this case, a subsequent granddaughter would be given this grandmother's name. Carrying this tradition over to America caused a problem for first-generation Americans. If the grandmother was Philomena, for instance, the granddaughter might be baptized Phyllis. If the grandfather was Antonio the grandson might be called Anthony.

Sometimes, children are named for Saints, typically for the Saint on whose Feast Day they were born, but sometimes for a Saint for whom the parents feel a special connection. Many Italian-Americans in the neighborhood celebrated not only your birthday but also your "names day" i.e. the day of the Saint you were name after. That was Saint Joseph in my case.

It was great for little children because it gave you two birthdays a year with two opportunities to receive gifts. I am sure that this is one custom that many children would like to bring back. It does remind me of a funny story about selecting my confirmation name while I was in grammar school.

It was a sunny afternoon and I was on my way back to St Gabriel's school for the afternoon session of my 3rd grade class when my classmate, Tony asked me if I had remembered to bring the note identifying my desired confirmation name back with me. The deadline was due today. I was to have my mother sign a paper agreeing to my Catholic Confirmation, a religious rite, which was to be held at the church in two weeks. This agreement slip also was to identify the confirmation name that I was to take as well. The ceremony was to be presided over by the Archbishop of Philadelphia.

I had forgotten to have my mother sign the paper. Now I knew I would be in trouble. The Nun would be very angry with me. It would be too late to go back home. I would be late for class if I did that.

I knew what I would do. I will sign the paper myself. Mom will never know. Sister will never know. There was only one problem. The paper also requires that you state a "confirmation name" for me. I know that my parents wanted my name to be "Henry" after my father's confirmation's name. It is the tradition. The problem is that I am not sure how to spell "Henry".

If I spelled it wrong, Sister Mary will know that it was not my mother who signed the paper. I asked Tony and he did not know how to spell "Henry" either. In fact, none of the guys knew. The solution was solved by placing "John" in the box and turning the paper into Sister that day. The weeks past and I heard nothing. I had gotten away with my deception.

The day of the Confirmation came. It was a beautiful sunny spring day. The entire neighborhood gathered in the Church. My parents sat in the front with the other parents dressed in their finest clothes. They were so proud. This was the Catholic ceremony that welcomed their boy into manhood. He was proclaiming his faith in God, as a man, in front of the whole community. The Archbishop traveled from center city to preside over the ceremony. It was a grand affaire.

The Archbishop then came to me and then pronounced me to be Joseph John Bonocore. You could see the astonishment on my father and mother's face. What happened to "Henry"? He was supposed to be Joseph Henry Bonocore.

My father and mother's patience that day taught me another great lesson in life. They were very disappointed in me but they took it in stride. It is another lesson that I will never forget.

VIA ARTE (Italian Street Painting)

Italian Street Painting has been an Italian tradition since the Sixteenth Century. The art of street painting is rooted in the religious heritage of Italian artists who once created art works in front of village churches during the long festival seasons. Folk artists, known as "madonnari," used rocks, pigment, and charcoal to decorate such town squares with images of the Madonna.

As the practice became an entrenched tradition in local festivals, artists began creating secular works that reflected popular artistic styles as well as religious iconography. Even today, The Italian village of Grazie di Curtatone continues to attract thousands of painters annually to its street painting celebration. In South

Philadelphia, many Italian-Americans children worked together to create streetscapes of vibrant color and texture.

Street painting is a temporary art medium in which artists use pastel chalk to create exciting and original works of art on asphalt since the artist's canvas is actually the street. The children used vivid colors and lots of imagination. They made their visions come alive as they design colorful works of art on the asphalt.

First Communion Dresses

One of the traditions in South Philadelphia is making a tailored First Communion dress for your little girl who would receive their First Communion in the local Parish. Since little girls first learn to talk in the neighborhood, their mothers would tell them about how beautiful they will be when they walk down the Church aisle in their communion dress to make their first communion. It would be one of those special times in their lives, like their wedding.

It was tradition that each little girl would have a dress especially made just for her and given to her by parents as a present to mark this special occasion. This tradition was started when Mrs., Savastano fashioned a pretty First Communion dress for her daughter. Other mothers liked it and requested dresses for their girls as well and the tradition began.

Soon she had a network of customers throughout the parish. As the girls grew up, they asked for prom dresses, and finally, one insisted she make a wedding dress. Mrs. Savastano protested her ignorance of the art, but the girl said, "Just pretend it's a white prom dress!" Word spread and Mrs. Savastano kept busy making communion dresses and wedding dresses for the next twenty years.

The Italian "Dressed Window"

One of the most widespread folk art traditions in the Philadelphia Italian neighborhoods today is the "dressed window". It is a display of ornaments and other items in a street-level rowhouse window. They are objects valued for their beauty such as porcelain vases, flowers, figurines and lace curtains inherited from the family's mothers and grandmothers that are placed in the home's front window and arranged in a decorative way.

In South Philadelphia, windows are recognized as art. Neighbors know who does a pretty window, and they imitate each other. Women in Italy traditionally assembled altars in their homes for holy images, family mementos, and one or two beautiful things. In South Philadelphia they do this with similar arrangements.

South Philadelphia windows have much in common from house to house. The family presents itself to the neighborhood through the items that it displays in its front window. The front window seems to give those that pass by a glimpse of both the family's individuality and it's acceptance of neighborhood's standards. Windows are also not dressed when a family is in mourning. The absence of anything in a window suggests that the people inside should be avoided, for example, children are told not to go trick-or-treating at houses without Halloween decorations.

My wife Phyllis in her First Communion Dress in May of 1955 in South Philadelphia

The Legend of the Tarantella

The Tarantella is the most popular of all the Italian songs and considered by many as the song of Italy. Its origin dates back to the Middles Ages and traces of a similar song can even be found in Magna Graecia. Legend states that between the 15th and 17th centuries an epidemic of tarantism swept through the town of Taranto in southern Italy as the result of being bit by the poisonous tarantula spider.

Once bitten the tarantata would fall into a trance that could only be cured by frenzied dancing. People would surround the victim while musicians would play mandolins, guitars and tambourines in search of the correct rhythm. Each beat would have a different effect on the tarantata causing various movements and gestures. Once the correct rhythm was found it was almost certain that the tarantata was cured.

Another version of the story states that a woman who was depressed and frustrated from the subordinate lifestyle would fall into a trance that could only be cured by music and dance. This lasted three days and during that time the tarantata would be the center of attention, which in turn would cure them of their frustrations and depressions.

Stick Ball

Stick ball is a game that rose from the streets of the urban cities and many an Italian-American boy grew up playing the game. No urban game carries more of a legend to an Italian-American boy growing up in the 20th century in the United States then stickball. I played this game for hours when I was a kid. As soon as school was out, we would go to the public school yard, one block from our house, and play until dark. We keep statistics by player and by team for the season. We were very serious about this game.

It was adapted from baseball and its' rules are closely linked to baseball. Stickball, transformed the urban landscape into a dramatic stage of competitions for the young Italian-American boys. Fantastic stories were told and retold of how games were won and played. Your street became the field. Lamp posts, car doors and manhole covers were the bases. Your neighborhood was the stadium and your neighbors were the fans. The building stoops were the seats for the fans and if the fans were looking out from windows and fire escapes that comprised the "upper decks."

Today there is even an actual Stickball Hall of Fame is located at the Museum for the City of New York. In it they have a virtual museum, telling the story of the athletes that played the game and teams that they honor. In addition to focusing on the players and games, they also tell stories about the neighborhoods that were part of this tradition.

When we played in our neighborhood, there were three basic forms of stickball: fast pitching against a wall, bounce pitching (also known as "slow-pitch" or "pitching in") and fungo (the baseball term describing the act of hitting the ball yourself). Fast-pitch, or wall ball, was played by 1 to 3 players per side in a schoolyard or parking lot where there's a big wall for the backstop and some open space for the field. Fungo and slow-pitch are usually played in the street, with anywhere from 3 to 8 players on a side.

In slow-pitch, a pitcher stands about 50 feet away from the hitter, and delivers a pitch lob that the hitter tries to clobber on a single bounce. Rules vary, but usually one, sometimes two strikes and you're out. Anything that lands on a roof is an automatic out. Anything that breaks a window or lands on a porch or area that gets you in trouble is also an automatic out (and probably "game over"). Besides that, regular baseball rules apply (running the bases).

Fungo is now the most common style currently played among organized stickball leagues. The basic style is to toss the ball up with one hand, hold the bat with the other. Let the ball bounce once, giving you enough time to shift into the proper batting stance. Just as it reaches the top, hit the ball.

In celebration of the Bronx's stickball tradition, Street play highlights great Bronx players and recalls the creation of "Stickball Blvd," the Bronx Street named after this urban tradition.

Box Baseball

Box baseball is another game that we played often. The ball is hollow inside and it lets you squeeze it to produce quite a bit of spin. The word "spin" might be an understatement, as those of you who have played this game might know. Box baseball provides a full baseball paradigm on a postage-stamp-sized field. You use three boxes. The pitcher leans in and pitches an underhand lob (with or without a spin) into the hitter's box. The batter straddles the box and tries to slap the ball into the pitcher's box, hoping it would not be caught.

Half ball

Another popular sport was half ball. As with the other games we have been discussing, half ball was also very popular in other Italian-American neighborhoods including Boston, St. Louis and parts of NYC. My friends and I would play it in the school yard for hours. Half ball was played like stickball, but the ball is cut in half. The ball is thrown with the same motion as skipping a rock across the water. The batter usually uses a broomstick for a bat. The batter gets one swing and a miss, if the catcher makes the catch in the air you are out.

If the catcher drops the swing and a miss the batter remains batting. Batted balls off walls or sides of gyms or buildings caught before they hit the ground are outs. Balls that are not caught will be awarded bases accordingly: double, triple, home run, depending where the balls are hit.

Marbles

We also played marble games in the streets with those cat-eyes, aggies, and alleys. Marbles is a street game people have been playing since before there were streets. The ancient Egyptians played games with small balls made of clay. In Renaissance Italy, glass blowers made glass "marbles" as children's toys. The first book about marbles was published in England in 1815.

The marbles you probably remember are the brightly-colored, machine-made glass marbles. The games we played were named Potsie, Forts, Ring Taw and Bossout. Like stickball, marble games have faded as a pastime, done in by asphalt paving, the rise of video games, and the death of the vacant lot.

TAROT

Italian women would spend many hours getting readings from the Tarot Card Readers. It seemed like a weekly habit for many people and they would swear by the results. Many of them would compare notes and talk about want came true and interpret want they thought came true.

The exact origins of the Tarot deck are shrouded in mystery. However, there is evidence that the first deck can be traced back to Italy in the mid 15th century. An Italian family by the name Visconti commissioned an artist, Bonifaco Bembo to paint a set of 78 cards as a wedding gift for his daughter. The cards were used to play a popular Italian gambling game called "Tarocchi".

In interviewing a neighborhood "reader", she explained: "The rationale for getting a reading remains the same over the last 500 years. People want answers to problems in their every day life. What you must remember when you do a reading is that the Tarot cards are not an infallible but in many cases you will predict your future".

"You must make of the interpretation what you want, the cards relate pictorially to what you are feeling. The cards can some times shed new light on a situation that you cannot see clearly due to being immersed in the emotion of the circumstances".

"The Tarot simply points out avenues or possibilities it is up to the questioner to act on the information."

Limoncello

Many people in the neighborhood liked the Italian drink called Limoncello. If you have ever been to Italy, you'll instantly know about limoncello. It is a lemon liqueur that is served well chilled in the summer months. It is wonderful as a palate cleanser or as an after dinner drinks.

You should keep your bottles of limoncello in the freezer until ready to serve. The ingredients are simple and making a batch doesn't require much work. Limoncello is the name for an Italian citrus-based lemon liqueur that is served well chilled in the summer months. Limoncello is now considered the national drink of Italy and can be found in stores and restaurants all over Italy.

It is the product acquired by the infusion of lemon skins in pure alcohol. I understand that it has become Italy's second most popular drink after Campari. It has long been a staple in the lemon-producing region along the Italian Amalfi Coast in Capri and Sorrento. The Amalfi Coast is known for its citrus groves and narrow winding roads. Authentic Limoncello is made from Sorrento lemons, which come from the Amalfi Coast. Families in Italy have passed down recipes for this for generations, as every Italian family has their own Limoncello recipe.

8

Italian Superstitions & Healers

This section discusses additional Italian-American superstitions. Italians are notorious for their superstitions. The most famous of which is the dark and intriguing "evil eye". But there are other superstitions as well that I remember from my time in the neighborhood. We will also discuss the neighborhood "healers" in this section as well.

THE "EVIL EYE"

Streghe, or Italian witches, were feared in South Philadelphia for their powers to give the evil eye, or il malocchio, to anyone who would cross them. The evil eye belief encompassed a range of phenomena, from malocchio (evil eye) to magical attacks, known as attaccatura fascino or legatura ("binding"), and fattura ("fixing"). It would be a supernatural punishment for which required a knowledgeable cure.

As legend goes, luckily there were cures for the "evil eye". Many of these cures required wearing amulets or devices around your neck. The most obvious of these is the phallus. The phallus was common in Roman art and sculpture, where its purpose was to bring good luck. This custom persisted in charms and amulets found throughout Italy well into the 20th century. It was usually carved in coral and was to be hung on a charm worn around the neck. Other phallic symbols such as fish, roosters, daggers, snakes and keys were also used protective amulets.

NEIGHBORHOOD "HEALERS"

In our neighborhood we also had a number of Italian women who were considered "healers" and many people in the neighborhood believed that they could cure a variety of illnesses. They used a number of remedies from herbs to magic formulas and prayers. There were professional sorcerers who were called in on serious cases where they believed that magical attacks had occurred.

In practice, however, each of these healers overlapped, since almost any illness could be judged as the work of any of these healers regardless of what they called themselves. Folk healers referred to themselves as streghe "witches", as fattuc-cchiere, "fixers," or maghi "magic-workers." Most of these healers inherited their craft from a relative since the tradition was that the power was handed down in the family.

According to a faith healer I talked to in South Philadelphia, she works in a state of trance. Usually the healer immerses herself in a dream-like state. While in this condition she amerces herself into a psychic condition with her client, and suffers with him/her. She starts crying and suffering along with her patient and sheds tears. If the healer does not weep, it means that she was not able to under-stand any spell in effect, and thus her client is not bewitched, and his illness is the result of other causes. Healers were consulted to discover whether an illness was caused by witchcraft, to find lost or stolen items, or for love magic. These people were also thought to posses healing knowledge, often in the form of magic for-mulas and prayers.

In South Philadelphia, the formulas are secret and proprietary; they belong to individuals in the community. Healing formulas were passed on from one family member to another at significant times of year such as Christmas Eve or St. John's Eve (June 23). The owner of the formula passes on the power along with the knowledge. Once they have been transmitted, the original owner ceases to practice. Often it is only certain family members who can receive the knowledge; for example, a descendent of the opposite sex, or the youngest daughter.

OTHER SUPERSTITIONS

I am told that many superstitions are still widely used in South Philadelphia today. For example, many young mothers in South Philadelphia still put their babies' undershirts on inside out. The explanations have changed. Instead of say-ing this is to keep away the evil eye. They now say the purpose of this custom is to protect babies' delicate skin from the chafing of the seams. But magic and occultism are not dead.

An 80 year old woman in the "old neighborhood" was a devout believer in the "evil eye." If she suspected someone was casting a "bad glance", she would tell us to place our thumb between our forefinger and our middle finger while making a fist. She told us that this will counteract the evil spell.

Another superstition that had it's roots in legend was to "knock on wood" The Italian tradition says that it originated with the notion that evil spirits, upon overhearing potential good news during human conversation, would try to sabotage the situation. The sound of rapping on wood was meant to keep the spirits from hearing the news as it was told.

It was told in the neighborhood that the custom of saying "God bless you" originated when someone sneezed and it was believed that a sneeze might accidentally expel a person's soul. For years, I watched my Mom toss a pinch of salt over her left shoulder after she would spill salt. The legend in the neighborhood is that the practice began when early man discovered the powers of salt for melting snow and preserving food, earning it a reputation as a positive talisman. Spilled salt was a warning from friendly spirits that evil was nearby, they reasoned. They threw salt over the left shoulder to appease the bad spirits that lived there. I guess the good spirits lived on the right.

As with many people, Italian-Americans are superstitious about the number 13. Triscadecaphobia is the fear of the number 13. Many believe Friday the 13th is especially a very unlucky day. In Ancient Rome, the citizens dedicated the 6th day of the week to their beautiful Goddess Venus. Eventually this day evolved into Friday, and was considered to be the luckiest day of the week.

Muslims claim Friday as the day Allah created Adam, legend has it that Adam and Eve ate the forbidden fruit on a Friday, and later died on a Friday. Christians consider Friday as the day on which Christ was crucified by the Romans. The Last Supper was where Jesus said goodbye to his apostles before being crucified. How many were at the table? 14, including Judas.

Next up was Friday, October 13, 1307. The Pope of the church in Rome in Conjunction with the King of France carried out a secret death warrant against "the Knights Templar". The Templar was terminated as heretics, never again to hold the power that they had held for so long. There Grand Master, Jacques DeMolay, was arrested and before he was killed, was tortured and crucified.

The Scandinavians believe that the number 13 signified bad luck came from their mythological 12 demigods, who were joined by a 13th demigod, Loki, an evil cruel one, who brought upon humans great misfortune. So, there are a number of reasons to find Friday the 13th an unlucky day.

9

Strong Family Values &
Community Relationships

I was born and raised in South Philadelphia which is the "Little Italy' of Philadelphia. Although I had a very difficult early life from an economic perspective, I have fond memories from my childhood. I look back on those years with great happiness from my birth in August of 1947 through the many events that shaped my life and molded me until I left South Philadelphia in 1969.

It is a trip that I was fortunate to have experienced and I look back on those years with warm feelings. Some sadness, yes, because those years are gone forever but also a joy that they gave me a good foundation to build my life. In this section, we will discuss some general comments about the Italian-American family, my family, the neighbors (who in many cases acted like family members), and family businesses (because they were so closely connected to the family). However, it is important to warn you that when you ask an Italian to tell you about his family, you better have a lot of time to hear the reply. They are very proud of their family and they have a lot of family members to talk about.

THE ITALIAN FAMILY

When many Italians think of their family they do not just think of their immediate family (i.e. wife and children). To the traditional Italian, the "family" included all those relatives whom most Americans would not consider when asking such a question, such as grandparents, uncles, aunts, cousins. In some cases, it would also include distant cousins. What we today would think of as the extended family today.

Also, based on centuries of experience, the Italians have learned that the family is not only a nurturing and loving unit for spiritual support but it is also an economic unit for helping to survive in this world. Each family member had a role to play and was expected to work, regardless of age, and contribute to common good of the needs of the family as a whole. Daughters and sons cleaned, cooked, gardened, and looked after their younger brothers and sisters. Children were seen as an economic resource and in the early immigration period they were seen as actually forced into schools until the age of 16.

One was not supposed to abandon his/her family. As a result, it was very difficult for an Italian American in the early years to attain a higher position on the social ladder. Also, in many Italian-American households in my neighborhood, aunts, uncles, cousins, and grandmothers often lived in the same house.

STORIES ABOUT MY FAMILY

I will start this story about our family with my grandfather. After returning from World War I, he regained his job at the factory. He married, and he and his wife had three sons. But the happy story ends there. His wife left him when the youngest of their three children, my father, was three years old. To this day, we do not know what happened. My grandmother may have returned to Italy. We just do not know. All three children were placed into an orphanage.

This story demonstrates some of the upheaval that was happening at that time in the neighborhood. There were a number of broken homes and a great need for orphanage services, like Mother Cabrini was providing, and foster care throughout the Italian immigrant community. There were very hard times for many of the families in the neighborhood including mine. But let me continue the tale with some so the stories that I remember starting with my grandfather.

STORIES ABOUT MY GRANDFATHER

My Grandfather, Antonio Bonocore was the patriarch of the family. Although he missed his beloved Italy very much, he enjoyed his new life in America and the friends he made here.

The Story Teller

When I was a child, my family and I would sit around the kitchen table with my grandfather talking for hours. My father would sit at his place in the corner by the window doing his crossword puzzle while we all talked. While dinner cooked on the stove, and steamed up the only window in the room, my mother would ask my brother and I about how our day in school was. But my grandfather would be telling us the stories about his days in the old country of Sicily.

My brother and I would listen attentively to my grandfather and soak it all in. I had all the questions. Here, while eating dinner, I learned about the town my grandfather was born in, his grandparents, and the joys and the hardships of growing up poor in Sicily. We heard about the earthquakes, the tempests, and the floods. We were taught about Saint Francis of Paola. And we heard about the mysterious superstitions. There was a delicate blend of good and evil. He told us about the cold winter nights his time in front of the fireplace and how they would eat cheese, suppresatta, and bread.

Sicily was a poor land yet no one ever went hungry. I was also born in a poor family in the United States but I felt so rich with tradition. My grandfather came to this country, penniless, but filled with ambition and hope for a better life.

After returning from World War I, my grandfather's wife left him and my father. Grandfather had no means to support them without a wife so he placed my father and his two brothers in an orphanage. He kept in touch with the three children through the years and each of the children was released from the orphanage at age sixteen to find jobs on their own. My father was the only son to gain a high school diploma, thanks to the family pitching in and carrying him for the extra year while he finished his education.

From there the Bonocores assimilated well into the American society. There were three families, and lots of cousins. They stayed in South Philadelphia and raised their families there. My uncle Tony worked hard all his life and has a heart as good as gold. He was always there when you needed him. He is the oldest brother and has been a rock when things have gone wrong in the family. The third brother, Uncle John is the second oldest child. John was also a very loving person. He passed away a few years ago. John will always be fondly remembered as a loving member of the family.

My Grandfather Antonio Bonocore in 1958

Home Made Italian Wine

"Good luck, for a hundred years," my grandfather's dinner guests shouted back. I remember how my grandfather's face beamed with pride at these happy occasions and each guest smiled as they sipped from the small glasses of red wine. Wine was always a part of our family's holiday meal. And, like most Italian-American kids, I was introduced to its flavor, at an early age.

Wine was present at each family celebration, baptisms, first holy communions, confirmations, birthdays, graduations and marriages. We also had wine with our meals on Sundays, holy days of obligation and all national holidays in my grandfather's apartment.

October is the traditional time of year for winemaking. It's the transition month between summer and fall, a time when grandfather gathered his equipment and ingredients to begin his task. Because we were on the east coast, my grandfather had to wait for good winemaking grapes to come in by rail car from California.

During the fall I can remember my grandfather making his annual trek down to Ninth Street in South Philadelphia to purchase grapes so he could make his own wine. He would come back with anywhere from 40-50 crates. My grandfather preferred red wine so he purchased purple grapes. He would make anywhere from 60-70 gallons of wine. He was proud of his wine and he would give it out to his family and friends during Christmas.

Once the grapes were purchased it was only a matter of time before he crushed them, which would begin the process of fermentation. Before we could begin the process all of the equipment needed to be scrubbed and washed. It is a painstaking, yet essential to the wine making process. Once everything was ready we would prepare to crush the grapes. My grandfather used a crusher, which would sit on top of this rather large wooden barrel. Devoted winemakers owned their own grape-crushers while others, like my grandfather, borrowed one each fall. After the crush was finished, the juice was poured by funnel into the huge oak barrels, which had been cured with sulfur smoke.

One by one he would begin to carry in the crates until he had all of them crushed. He usually filled three to four wooden barrels. Once they were crushed the grapes would remain in the barrels and each night my Dad or he would go down and use a long piece of wood to push the grapes down. While he was making wine, my mother was hard at work making pastas and sausages in preparation for dinner.

In the fall, I watched as the family gathered in the cellar to cure the wine barrels and I helped my father and grandfather set up the winepress. I remember helping my father and grandfather haul in the grapes; and set up the grape-crusher and watch as the grapes cured in the oak barrels. My grandfather said that wine has been made in some regions of Italy since 1000 C.E. It was a standard of Chianti that grandfather tried his best to clone. When they were crushed the grapes would stay in the barrels and each night he would go down to squeeze the grapes down. Within three weeks it was time to press the grapes and fill the five gallon glass jugs with the wine.

The jugs were capped and they would sit in the cellar. This would allow the sediment to settle to the bottom. It has been some time since I have had an opportunity to take part in this tradition. Since the passing of my grandfather, the tradition stopped, but my memories did not. Then the talent for good wine-making began. One mistake and the winemaker's barrels would be filled with vinegar instead of wine. But, like grandfather, most winemakers had inherited their skills from the Old Country and rarely made a bad batch.

Ninth Street

I would also enjoy watching my grandfather when he did his serious food shopping on Ninth Street. As a young boy I would accompany him and help carry the shopping bags back to my parent's house by bus on a Saturday morning. One of my earliest memories was to see my grandfather buy a live chicken. The chicken would be slaughtered, plucked, cleaned and wrapped in a minute or two. When I would walk down Ninth Street with my grandfather, he would tell me the story of how it reminded me of the marketplace in his hometown in Sicily.

He would tell me how a Sicilian street market is a cacophony of sights and sounds. It would be a colorful assortment of fruits, vegetables, fish and meats to vendors barking about bargains to anybody who will listen. The ambience would be punctuated by colored tarpaulins suspended as "tents" to protect the wares from the elements. Italian and foreign items would vie for your attention. There would be tarocchi (blood oranges), giri (leafy greens), chicory, herbs, artichokes, cuttlefish, swordfish, prawns, gutted goats, lambs, breads and cheeses.

He told me that Sicily's outdoor market tradition dates from the ninth-century Saracen rule of the island He said the weather was always beautiful. Outdoor vendors would be in coastal cities where it hardly ever gets cold enough to snow. Almost every town and urban neighborhood has its "mercatino" ("little market") that opened at least once a week. Especially in Palermo where the open air markets occupy narrows medieval streets. He told me that some of the outdoor markets stand on the very same sites today as they did in the tenth century.

<u>Sicilian Puppets Collection</u>

Grandfather had a small collection of Sicilian Puppets. They would sit on the table in his living room and I would play with them every time I visited his home when I was a child. They were one of the few treasures that he brought with him from his home in Sicily. He was very fond of those puppets and they had a special meaning to him.

My research suggest that the origin of Sicilian Puppets suggest they where probably brought to Sicily from the Spain of Don Quixote. Initially, the Sicilian Puppets represented a dialectic and dramatic interpretation of Sicilian history and their folk-culture. They demonstrated expression of a person's aspirations with respect to power, justice, and the world.

Grandfather told me how he would watch them perform in outside theaters in Sicily. In those shows, the Sicilian Puppets acted out the people's dilemma between being faithful or not, Christian or pagan. The puppets were a great way to demonstrate to the children the constant battles between "good vs. evil" and 'right vs. wrong". They were a constant reminder of his family and his early days in Sicily.

<u>The Best Cook in the Family</u>

Grandfather also told me that the French loved Italian cooking so much, that when Napoleon invaded Italy, they took Italian wives and chefs back to France with them. That is how great French cuisine was born. Now you can find Italian influences in nearly every type of cuisine throughout the world. I do not know if that is true or not but it is a great story to tell your Italian-American grandchildren.

My grandfather was the best cook in the family. I can remember the Sundays that we all would go over to his apartment to have Sunday dinner. Many times he would be cooking a very simple dish because he knew it was my favorite. It was meatballs in tomato sauce. I would enter the kitchen and inhale the smells from the stove as the sauce and the meatballs were cooking and I would wait impatiently for dinner to begin.

He would let me taste the meatballs and sauce before the meal and it would make me feel very special. I was the official taster and I was the one who would determine when the meal was ready to be served.

He would take me aside each time and tell me how his mother would teach him all her recipes. She would tell him how important it was for boys to know how to cook as well as girls. "Cooking is a basic skill", she would say to him. "Learn in well". To this day, I still cook on at least Christmas Day and Thanksgiving Day for my family.

My Grandfather: The Bocce Star

I would also spend hours with my grandfather at the local Bocce Club watching him play for his team. He was somewhat of a local star in the neighborhood. Bocce is an Italian-American sport that can be played at the professional level or enjoyed by the family in the backyard during a family outing. It is a great way to time together with your relatives.

I would be proud of him, as he would lead his team to a win almost every time I saw him play. As I look back on it, I do not remember his team losing a game but I am sure they did. Their bocce club was only five blocks from my house so I would walk over to the club on many occasions to see him and watch the games.

His friends knew me and asked me if I would play bocce when I grew up. I never did join the club. I spent my time with baseball and football and all the American sports. I know it disappointed my grandfather but I never did seem to have time to spend with him at the Bocce Club when I grew older. Now that he is gone, I wish I had spent more time with him there.

STORIES ABOUT MY MOM

My mother and father married in 1946 when he returned from the Army at the end of World War II. I was born in 1947 and my brother in 1949. Our third brother, Mark, was not born for another 17 years. My mother Marie (b.1927) was born and raised in South Philadelphia as was my father Joseph, nicknamed "Joe (b. 1923). My mother was one of eight children (two brothers and six sisters). My father was one of three brothers.

My mother's family was from northern Europe and had been in the United States for a few generations earlier. Both families settled in South Philadelphia. Mom insisted that we get the best education we could. She would spend her nights working with my brothers and me on our homework making sure that we understood our work. She was determined that each of us would go to college and receive a college diploma and we all did.

My mother also strictly followed Solomon's advice, in never sparing the rod; in so much that I have frequently been whipped for looking blue on a frosty morning. Mom whipped us for the right things. We did get out of hand many times but it did teach us discipline. My mother said that one mustn't spoil children.

Dad, Mom and I on my Senior Prom Night in 1965

The Chef of the House

Although Mom was not Italian, my grandfather taught my mom how to cook. He taught her the "Italian Way". Mom learned to cook from sight, smell and feel. This is the authentic method of old world Roman cooking. She spent my childhood in the kitchen making everyday meals, but also the holiday dishes she would prepare for the large groups of relatives who would gather in our dining room throughout the year.

School friends and my Dad's work buddies alike often meet for home-cooked dinners, during which she would proudly present her recipes and they would also comment on my grandfather's wine. There was always individual budget limits on the choice of food and beverage, but everyone shared the same enthusiasm for her food while they shared strong opinions at the dinner table over politics or other topics of the day. One of the greatest myths must be that all Italian sauces are red. While many Southern Italian dishes do use tomatoes, there are so many other dishes that we had while I was growing up in South Philadelphia that do not involve pasta or even sauce.

We were a typical South Philadelphia Italian-American family. The menu for the week was actually quite simple. On Sunday mom would make the Meat Sauce with pasta, Monday was usually steak night or some type of meat, Tuesday she would have the sauce leftover from Sunday over fresh pasta.

Wednesday she would cook veal cutlets (another treat when we could afford them) or some other meat again. Thursday we ate that same sauce and pasta from Sunday (she usually made it in big batches), Friday she made real homemade pizza with anchovies or tuna fish sandwiches (old school) Italians NEVER eat meat on Friday, even if it's not Lent). Saturday we would go out for dinner (at a diner) or it is more sauce with pasta.

Many times, on a Saturday afternoon, mom would make her recipe for the famous traditional Italian Beef Sandwich. It was delicious and I can still taste it when I think about sitting around the kitchen table and waiting for her to make the sandwiches for us to eat. It was made with thinly sliced roast beef, mayonnaise, fresh rosemary, horseradish, and arugula on a baguette. You should try it sometime on a lazy Saturday afternoon.

You could predict every day what you were going to have for dinner. It was just like everything else in the Italian-American community—a tradition!!!

Mom's Time with Us

Mom's bedtime stories to her children were rarely read from a book. Instead, they were real-life events and adventures from her childhood, adventures that fed my own creativity and imagination. Her nightly yarns were made up of little family histories and stories. It was the family's habit to always attend church on Sundays and holy days' of obligation. There were days when I wanted to stay home and play. If I wanted to stay home, the answer from my mother was always the same: "Out of our habits grow our character on our character we build our destiny." This was the code Italian American immigrants lived by and why they found success in America.

St. Joseph's Day Dinner

I remember that my mother always invited people to dinner when she first met them. She inherited that from my father. When people of Italian decent first meet each other it is customary that one invite the other to dinner. It is a gesture of friendship. Mom followed this custom even though she was not Italian but she felt like she was since she was adopted into the Italian culture when she married my father.

Her generosity was also extended on holidays as well. One that I remember especially was on my names day, St. Joseph, or San Giuseppe, who is called "the just man". St. Joseph is the patron saint of home life, of fathers, and of a happy death. On St. Joseph's feast day, March 19th, a meal of a minimum of thirteen meatless, cheese less dishes is prepared. Mom would usually invite a number of new friends to dinner on this occasion each year.

The dinner is offered to express gratitude to the saint for protecting and aiding the family in the previous year. Fish is not excluded from the meal, which has dishes of codfish and salmon, specially prepared bread, beans, vegetables, pasta, desserts, wine, minestrone soup, and Zeppole di San Giuseppe, the traditional honey and flour fritters dusted with ground almonds and candied orange peel.

The tradition was that three of those in attendance are chosen to represent Mary, Joseph and Jesus. The dishes were brought out one by one, with the three characters having the first tastes of each. At the end of the dinner, each guest takes something home and whatever is left is taken to the local poor. This is to emulate the first feast of St. Joseph, which was offered in thanks for the saint's answer to prayers for rain during a Sicilian drought.

The Weekly Hospital Visits With My Father

It was a cold Sunday in 1960 when I accompanied my 32-year-old mother to the Hospital in Valley Forge, Pennsylvania. Mom never missed a weekly visit with my Dad. This labor of love continued for four years. My father was in the hospital with tuberculosis in the lungs and he had undergone two operations and various therapies. She was there supporting him every week throughout it all.

Entering the Hospital each week was often a replay of all our previous visits over the years. We saw the same patients every time we visited. Many had the same look with pale faces and hollow eyes and as each of their bodies shook. It broke my heart to see them each time I visited. Then there was the eerie silence in the hospital that always had a profound effect upon me. There was always so much activity yet it was done with so little noise. You always wondered how they managed to keep the place so quite.

My father always presented himself in a happy mood although we knew that he wanted to be home. Hand-in-hand my mother and he would walk around the grounds of the hospital talking about the family. That day, we walked slowly across a snow-cleared road to a wooden picnic table encrusted in a blanket of ice. We would usually have a picnic and mom would bring out a pot of her home-made Italian cooking. We would eat and talk for hours about the good times we had as a family and what it will be like when dad is better and he is released from the hospital and returns home.

Mom would cry each time the visit was over but we would then look forward to next Sunday and know that we will see him again. We also knew that, with God's help, he would get well, and he would return to the family soon.

Stories about Dad

My father was a Saint of a man. I loved him very much. I miss him every day. He lived a very difficult life on earth. Beginning with his early childhood in the orphanage and during his later life he had a series of debilitating illnesses. When I was ten years old, he was diagnosed to have tuberculosis. He was an arc welder (steelworker) and worked in a hazardous work area all his life and it finally caught up with him.

He spent the next four years in the hospital in upstate Pennsylvania. At that time a patient with in his condition was expected to be quarantined and could not be allowed home until completely cured. As you would expect, this caused the family significant emotional and financial hardship for years. My mother and I supported the family (can you imagine a ten year old with a job?), while my father fought to regain his health. I could see the frustration in my father's eyes each time we visited him because he couldn't support his family but I never saw anger. Instead I saw a man with ambition. I saw a man with a sense of humor.

The South Philadelphia community helped us in our hour of need. One example was in saving our house from being foreclosed. The story is as follows.

When I saw my mother crying one day, I asked her why she was so sad. She explained to me that she had received a foreclosure notice on the house because we were behind in the house payments on the mortgage.

I walked down to the local bank and talked to the Vice President in charge of the branch. I explained our situation to the Vice President who was an Italian who lived in the neighborhood and was a member of our church. He took our mortgage papers out of the filing cabinet and put them in his desk draw. He told me he would keep them there until I came back to him when we could afford to start up our payments again. He told me to come back to him as soon as we could afford to start paying the bank our mortgage and I did.

This was just one example of how close the community was in those days. Another example is how my Aunt Doris and Uncle Bill drove our family for two hours each weekend to visit our father in the hospital when we did not have a car. They gave up their weekends and did this for four years. The neighbors and my father's co-works also helped us financially and emotionally for the entire time my father was out of work. Surly, I thought that with the passing of time it would make them forget us but they did not.

These are real examples of the Italian-American value system in action.

Dad in front of our house in 1962

<u>The Diner</u>

Another story about my father happened in the local diner and it came at a pivotal time in my life. As with many 18 year old boys, I was a senior ready to graduate high school with my whole life ahead of me. The friends that I "hung out with" at the diner were not interested in college. My mother urged me to go to college for years but I was having second thoughts under great peer pressure and the desire to make some fast money.

My father walked into that diner, unannounced, one night and had a heart to heart conversation with me that I will never forget. There, in front of all my friends, we discussed his disappointments in life, how he wished he had gone to college and how better off I would be in the long term if I went to school. That discussion was one of those father and son moments that changed my life since it was there I decided to apply to the University. I will remember that conversation forever.

Christmas Eve with My New Non-Italian Girlfriend

I brought a date to my parents' house one Christmas Eve when I was sixteen years old. I thought it would be interesting for a non-Italian girl to see how an Italian family spends the Christmas holidays. The year was a good one and so we had a feast that year. I thought my father and my date would hit it off. Boy, I was wrong!

I had only known Margaret for a month when I asked her to join us for dinner. I told her that it could be a little uncomfortable but if she did not mind it might be fun to see how an Italian-American family celebrates the Holidays. I told her, "My folks are great, we have a lot of fun on Christmas Eve." I told my father and mother that I was bringing Margaret for dinner. They said that they were looking forward to meeting her. What more could I want? We were on the right tract. They were receptive to meeting her.

In an Italian home, Christmas Eve is one of the social events of the year. My mother cleaned the house, cooked the dinner, and baked for days in preparation for the event. She prepared every minute of the entire evening. Christmas Eve is one of the events that every Italian family live for each year. I never realized that Margaret was the type of women that make Italian men like my father go crazy. But during the night we found that out.

After we arrived, Margaret and I waited for a half hour for the other family to arrive. In that time, my father determined that Margaret does not clean, cook, or bake. I should have arrived with her much later in the evening.

When the other family arrived, we sat around the dining room table for antipasto, which is a platter of lettuce, roasted peppers, black olives, anchovies, lunch meats, and cheeses. Mom offered Margaret some of the antipasto but she declined saying that she did not like anchovies or roasted peppers. My father looked at me with a very strange stare. When the traditional Christmas Eve seven fishes were served, Margaret declined by saying "I don't like fish" to all the different types of baked and boiled seafood on the table. My mother made the sign of the cross.

My father asks Margaret what her family eats on Christmas Eve. And Margaret said, "Ham." My father was beside himself and did not know what to say. This was not turning out the way I had expected. The night continued though coffee and dessert with Margaret and my family feeling very much out of place and uncomfortable with each other throughout the rest of the night.

It may come as a surprise to you, but my relationship with Margaret ended soon after that night. It seemed that we had very little in common. I wonder if that dinner had anything to do with it. What do you think?

Dad's War Buddy

I remember one of my father's stories about his time in World War II and one of his Italian-American buddies. I think this story demonstrates the value of commitment to your country as well as commitment to your friends. It also shows how my father valued him as a friend though all those years.

The event happened in France during heavy fighting with the German Army. My father was sharing a foxhole with a soldier who was hit with shrapnel. The soldier refused to be evacuated for treatment after he was hit. He wanted to stay and fight rather then leave his fellow soldiers. My father knew that he was wounded badly and that he should have gone for treatment but no one was going to change the soldier's mind. The fighting continued for another hour or so and then it happened. My father saw his friend laying there motionless. He was dead.

My father was very impressed with his friend's dedication to duty, and devotion to him, and his fellow soldiers. He had given his life when he could have chosen not to. If he had gone for treatment that day, he may still be alive, but he chose to stay and fight with his buddies.

My Father: A True Inspiration

My Dad is with me in spirit every time I wake up in the morning or go to bed at night. I remember each time we talked as we played chess together. I think of him when I turn on the television. I think about how we would watch a ball game together. When I hear the announcer say, "Strike three, you're out," I immediately think of him. I could see us together watching the game and having a great time as we rooted for the Philadelphia Phillies to win. His eyes would sparkle as he would laugh at the missed pitch and praise the Phillies pitcher for the good fastball. If I close my eyes, I can still see him now.

Dad was not a big man, about 5'9" tall and about 160 lbs but he was a giant to me. At the time, he was the wisest man that I ever knew. He was always reading a book and we were always talking about exotic things. History was his favorite subject to talk about but we would talk about just anything. Science, math, economics, philosophy etc. He was well read in it all.

Despite the fact that he had only a high school education and he was raised in an orphanage, he had this thirst for knowledge that seemed to be unending. I would spend hours with him learning as much as I could about as many subjects as I could. It was sad that we never did get to spend the time together that we should have. He was away from the family for those years while he was ill with tuberculosis and he was bed-ridden with cancer for the last four years of his life. He died when he was fifty-six years old.

I will never forget the day he died. I was on a business trip to London. I was in a business meeting and, at the exact time of his death, I had this strange feeling come over me that something terrible had happened. It was frightening. At the end of the meeting I returned to the hotel and my wife told me that we received a call from my brother Bob who said that my father passed away.

STORIES ABOUT BOB

Robert (Bob) Bonocore was my younger brother who was born in May of 1949. Bob and I were born twenty months apart. We were so close in age that we experienced almost everything together while we were growing up. However, Bob was more artistic and creative then I was. He was always writing stories and drawing pictures. I, on the other hand, was the brother who was always ready to play baseball instead.

The School Desk

One afternoon in June, eleven year old Bob was walking down our street coming from school carrying a desk. The desk was bigger then he was. Many neighbors were looking at him wondering why he was carrying this desk home from school.

Once Bob reached the house, my Mom saw the desk and was amazed that he had waked the mile from St. Gabriel's School to our home with it. But once she got over that, the next question was even more basic. Why?

Brother Bob at his First Communion in 1956

Bob went on to explain that his teacher, the nun, had been inspecting the school's desks in preparation for the end of the school year. She found many marks and scratches on Bob's desk. It was not acceptable and the desk had to be repaired for use by the next student in next year's class. She sent it home with

Bob so the nicks would be sanded out and the desk would be varnished for next year's use. She explained to Bob that the desk was in his possession for the year so that it was his responsibility to repair it.

Bob, in the dutiful Italian-American tradition, spent the weekend rubbing out the scratches and varnishing the desk. On Monday, he, with the help of my Mom, returned the desk to St. Gabriel's as good as new. It was in great shape for the student that would use that desk the next year.

Choosing Sides in Baseball

When playing neighborhood baseball games, the kids would begin by "choosing sides" or picking the members of the teams. You would begin by selecting a captain and he/she would start by selecting the first player to be on their team. They would then take turns selecting each kid one at a time until all kids were chosen and then the game would begin.

Usually, the younger children would be chosen last because of their less developed athletic skills but that never bothered Bob. Rather then play with children his age, he would always choose to play with me and my friends who were three years older and much more athletically advanced when we played sports. But rather then be the star at his age group, he would prefer to be chosen last in our "pick up' games and play with us.

He would play his heart out and he enjoyed the game very much. In the end, I think it made him a much better player. This story tells you a lot about Bob.

Brothers in Bad Times

Bob and I shared a lot of emotional moments when Dad was away in the hospital for all those years. As young children, we were going through a very emotional time and we were not sure how we were expected to act in the situation. We knew that we still had our mother at home with us but she was very unhappy and we could see that she was very uncertain of what she should do next.

We were always told that we could be anything that we want to be if we work hard enough and put our mind to it. Apparently that was not always true. Bob and I saw that our Mom and Dad worked as hard as anyone we knew and look at the situation that they were in now. He had a terrible illness. She was about to loose the house and we did not know where we were going to live or go to school. Ultimately we got through it all together as a family.

My bother and I grew very close during that time. Through those difficult experiences, we vowed that we would remain close and help each other throughout our lives. We have remained close up to this day.

STORIES ABOUT MY WIFE PHYLLIS

Teenage Dating & Meeting Phyllis

Phyllis is an Italian-American who was born and raised in South Philadelphia also. She graduated from Saint Maria Goretti High School. You can tell from reading this book that we share a number of common experiences but one of the most vivid in both of our memories is our wedding.

Many of the Italian couples who were married in South Philadelphia met at Bishop Neumann High School's Saturday Night Dance. Most Catholic boys attended Bishop Neumann High School and most the Catholic girls attended Saint Marie Goretti High School. Phyllis and I were the exception; we meet at a high school football game. The Saturday Night Dance was our second date.

Teens gathered together on the weekends at the dance on Saturday night at Bishop Neumann High and the High School football game wherever it was played on Sunday afternoons. We would enjoy parting in groups. This social approach made us feel less pressure. It would also allow newcomers to the group to get to know us faster without undue pressure. It also gave the parents a sense of security knowing their son or daughter is not alone or with a stranger.

The innocence and reputation of Italian-American girls in those days was always carefully protected, and it was in the best interests of the men in the neighborhood that bad words not get around about him. When you are part of an Italian-American family, your sex talk with you father is a lot more then just about the "birds and the bees". Dad also gave me an in-depth lecture on the requirements of a future spouse. La futura sposa italiana needed to be attractive but she needed to be much more.

Dad said that a wife also had to be able to enter into and contribute to the family. Italian men would seek a future business partner who was physically strong and a companion willing to work with her hands. Women who were reluctant to work with their hands, as some were, would have difficulty getting married—unless, of course, they came from very wealthy families. In many cases, in Italian marriage proposals your physical capabilities as related to farm work might be valued more highly than your outward appearance or looks.

Our Italian Wedding

When I asked Phyllis's father for her hand in marriage, I felt like it was a corporate merger. At a certain point during the transaction, I had to produce a diamond ring for Phyllis and ask for her hand in marriage. Believe me, the bigger the diamond ring; the better. The size of the diamond is a symbol of honor. This would give financial security and a comfort zone to Phyllis' family and prove the earnestness of the pretendente (future groom), giving him increased likelihood of having his offer accepted.

Mr. Donze (Phyllis' father) was instrumental in helping me meet and get to know their family but that is not an easy task in a big Italian-American family where everyone wants to have a say in the upcoming wedding. He would, at one time, not only verify my background but also take care of any and all marriage formalities. I was happy that he did not employ the services of a matchmaker; the responsibility always remained on the parents shoulders.

Even today it is not uncommon for the girl's parents to investigate carefully all available information regarding a suitor and his family. All relatives going back for several generations can be checked. Sometimes police records can be looked into. And of course, the local gossip at the neighborhood bar serves as an unlimited source of information.

Phyllis & I leaving the Church after Our Wedding

Phyllis, like many other girls in South Philadelphia, was in the habit of collecting household items and clothing in a hope chest as women did in many parts of the world. Her family also had a little dowry or money at the time of marriage.

In Italy, hope chests had to be very carefully packed and left in special hiding places, because during the next war, and there were several in Italy, where the soldiers of an invading army coming through might walk in and take out its carefully selected contents.

I also remember our Church services very well. During our ceremonies a large bowed ribbon was stretched across the top of the doorways of the Catholic Church to indicate that someone was getting married at the parish that day. As the Italian tradition, we were showered by rice and paper confetti as we came out after the church ceremony to greet everyone. Confetti represented money and good fortune and that is why an awful lot of confetti came showering by all the surrounding well wishers as we exited the church.

You can always tell how important or well-respected (not necessarily how wealthy) our parents were by attendance at the wedding reception. Our parents must have been well respected because it seemed that most of South Philadelphia was at the reception. There must have been three hundred people in the small hall at 10th and Snyder Avenue. I think they had to turn people away because they could not fit in the hall.

We had a very formal wedding reception after the ceremony in the church so our family and friends could celebrate the festive occasion with us. Before any food was served, I greeted the guests at the reception with a tray of liquor, sweet liquors for the women and strong drinks for the men. The toast was said: "Cent Anni" literally means "100-years" as if to say, 100 years of live, love and happiness.

The Dinner contained more than a dozen courses. Many symbolized specific foods for good luck. One was "starter' Wedding Soup, which is actually chicken soup with miniature meatballs. Espresso and pastries were served after the dinner, and of course, once everyone has had enough to eat and drink the Tarantella dance!

As is the Italian tradition, Phyllis carried a satin bag called la borsa. Our guests greeted her throughout the night and placed envelopes containing money into that bag as a wedding present. One thing I remember from my childhood about Italian weddings, are those sugar-coated almonds in plastic mesh bags which are called bomboniera. They are to symbolize the "bitter-sweet" sacrament of marriage. The odd numbers are luckier to the Italians, so there should always be an odd number of these candies. Also, when you serve your sambuca with coffee beans, 3 is traditional, again, always an odd number.

The traditional Italian wedding cakes are usually multi-layered with two little figures at the very top representing the bride and groom and we had it. These two plastic representations appear smiling and looking over with approval in the direction of all the guests at the reception. Our wedding cake was a seven layer Italian Rum Cake.

At the reception, my brother, after about his fourth glass of wine got up and said these words in a loud and excited voice: "evviva gli sposi" ("hurray for the newlyweds"). This triggered a thundering applause from everyone and many well wishing comments and the celebration continued. When it would slow down, one of my ushers got up and shouted once more "evviva gli sposi" and the crowd will respond with another round of applause. Next, as in any predictable series of events some Old Italian man said bacio, bacio…or "kiss, kiss, we want a kiss". Then Phyllis slowly and reluctantly stood up and obliged the audience.

We then followed the Italian tradition that may still exist for some couples today. We shatter a glass. The number of pieces that remain is supposed to represent the years of happiness we will have together.

Wedding receptions are not over until all the guests feel so full they need someone to carry them home in a wheelbarrow. Joyful Italian songs and wedding music were played while the guests ate away the best that South Philadelphia had to offer, chatting about politics, economics and the Phillies (the local professional baseball team). Meanwhile, as the wedding reception began to wind down, we made a slow round of all the tables to greet everyone.

Afterwards, we quietly and inconspicuously left for the honeymoon vacation without even opening a single wedding gift and our formal Italian wedding was over.

Phyllis & I kissing during the Reception

The Donze Family Picnics

Phyllis's parents, Tony & Mary Donze would have picnics two or three times a year for the immediate family. Only the closest relatives would be invited to their home for the Italian barbeque and fiesta. If my memory serves me correctly, usually 90 to 100 close relatives would attend each event. As you can tell, they tried keeping the affair small. One event would usually be held at the beginning of the summer and another would be held at the end of the summer.

The main athletic event at the picnic was the bocce competition, which each time resulted in the crowning of the various family champions in the different age groups. One great thing about the sport of bocce is that you can play it at any age and even in almost any physical condition. You also can play it on any field. No special set up is necessary. It is a great sport to get 100% participation.

The purpose of the game is to roll the bocce, a 4½ inch ball weighing about three pounds, as close as possible to the pallino, a 1¾ inch ball which is rolled down the alley first. The bocce that is closest to the pallino scores. Twelve points constitute a game.

Some authorities claim the game Bocce originated in Egypt about 5200 B.C.; others, that the game was started in Greece during the 6th Century B.C. The most reliable sources agree that Bocce, as we know it today, was played between battles during Rome's Punic Wars against Carthage, which started in 264 B.C.

Each summer, after eating the great meal, the family would divide up by age groups. They would then take turns playing bocce until a winner(s) was (were) crowned. The bocce games were fun. Thinking of them brings back great memories of how the family enjoyed spending time together.

Some members of the Donze family getting ready for the Donze picnic in 1952: Center is Grandfather Nunzio, my wife Phyllis & Rick Donze are on his lap, Joe is next to Phyllis, Bob is next to Rick, Left to right the adults are Aunt Florence, Tony (Phyllis' Dad), Aunt Lucy, & Mary (Phyllis's Mom)

<u>My Wife Phyllis's Grandmother</u>

From when she came to America from Italy, her life was dedicated to helping her family and her community. Since she spoke in "broken English" we all had a great time having fun understanding her at times but she was a sweet and caring person. Grandma also helped a number of her friends from the "old country" come to America. She aided them by giving them a place to stay if they need it.

Grandma's admirable determination and deep spirituality was responsible for her incredible zest for life. She had a faith in God and love of her family that strengthened her will. She had strong beliefs, which helped her through many adversities. She had a rough childhood and living through the Great Depression made her one of the best teachers of life to her family.

Grandma loved to tell stories and it was one of her grandchildren's favorite pastimes. Some stories were told with humor, while others showed a little drama. And she was an avid fan of the Philadelphia Phillies. At age 70, she would walk miles to the ballpark to see a baseball game and root for the team to win a game. She knew the batting averages of all the ball players until the day she died at 90 years of age. She was a real baseball fan.

Despite her spunky and opinionated demeanor, the staunch democrat was known to shout about her distaste of government policies, and criticize Republican politicians. If she disagreed with you, you would know it! Phyllis's grandmother also never turned away from a debate. She always used her outspoken viewpoint and stubbornness to help others too. Whether the cause was a church dinner or raising money for a sick member of the community she was a giving person who used her abilities to help. Her incredible spirit is still the topic of conversation at family gatherings even years after her death. That is another measure of your true value in life.

The picture of Phyllis & Her Grandmother was taken at Christmas time and was special to both of them

STORY ABOUT AUNT DORIS

Through the years, I've come to rely upon my aunt Doris, my mother's sister, as a fountain of endless family histories, anecdotes and generational stories. Whenever I've needed facts, details and dates on the subject of family milestones and histories, it was my aunt Doris, the family matriarch, whom I've called upon for my mom's side of the family. She told me one family story that I think demonstrates the nature of the South Philadelphia caring for others.

I mentioned that my mother and Doris come from a big family. One day, a strange man knocked on their door and told them that he was their distant uncle of my grandmother who had just arrived from Europe and had no place to live.

Aunt Doris & Uncle Bill were second parents to me

Despite the fact that their parents lived in a small home with six small children at the time, they took him. He lived with them for three years until he got on his feet in the United States.

This man has long past away and, to this day, no member of our family can verify if he was ever truly an uncle of my grandmother. Yet, he was warmly brought into the family and taken care of only on his word. Imagine that happening today.

STORIES ABOUT OUR NEIGHBORS

Our Neighbor Adopts a Grandfather

One of our neighbors adopted a grandfather. Yes, that is right. They adopted a grandfather. An old gentleman who lived down the street lost his wife. His wife was all he had left in the world. Their only son had died in World War II. The old man was retired and he was now living alone with his wife's cat in their small row home.

The remaining relatives that he did have were in Italy. He would get out each day to go to the store. He would also get out on a periodic basis to the doctors, pharmacy and to do his laundry. The idea for the adoption came from the children of the neighbors. The children loved the old man. They have been playing with the old man for years when they would see him in the neighborhood.

The old man has played stickball and football with them in the street as well as other games. He was also there when the kids needed help on many occasions. He would sit on the steps with them and tell them stories about Italy and other exotic places. They went to their parents and asked why the old man could not stay with them. They knew he was lonely in that house by himself and many of the other houses on the street had old people in them. "Why don't we have an old person in our house too"? The parents agreed and the story had a happy ending with the family adopting a grandfather and it brought a richer dimension to the children's lives.

Neighborhood Sausage Maker

Another fond memory is the neighbor who was the sausages maker. I guess that sausage-making is a fading craft. Part of the reason may be because there are not very many butchers practicing anymore. With the age of supermarkets, there is not much of a need for sausage maker anymore. He came from Naples, Italy, and opened a small meat market in the 1930s, serving the South Philadelphia neighborhood. He scaled back the business to making sausages just for local shops and neighbors in the 50s and moved to a tiny storefront.

That is when his daughter learned to make Italian sausages alongside her father. While he cut and mixed, Rosa taught herself how to trim, grind, and stuff the meat. She's never lived more than a few blocks from her family's business.

After he died Rosa carried on the business for a while, but she found it too much of a burden while also raising her son.

You can still buy sausage in South Philadelphia but not like theirs. I wonder where the good old sausage makers are today. It seems like a dying art.

Our Neighbor's Trip to Tuscany

It was very exciting in the neighborhood when someone in the neighborhood returned from a trip to Italy. Most of our family and friends were poor and the trip was very expensive so it was very seldom that you knew someone who could actually go there.

When one of our neighbors and his family took a trip one summer to Tuscany it was the talk of the neighborhood. We could not wait for their return to hear all about their adventure and to learn about the country and what news they could bring us. Before they left, they were give a list of people to contact who were relatives of all the neighbors. They were given letters to deliver in case they did contact those people. It was a very exciting experience even before they even left on their journey.

Upon their return, the stories of their adventure were fantastic. They talked about a train ride from Milan to Cumo. They talked about staying with relatives in Siena, Tuscany. They described the drive through Tuscany as beautiful; the rolling mountains as being so plush and how they look like velvet.

They described Siena as a beautiful old town, located in the mountains, with beautiful old houses and large Public Square. Each year the town hosts "The Palio" which is a horse race around the square. Each horse is sponsored by one of the Italian families in the area. It is a major event, which draws thousands of people and brings honor to the winning family.

Today, we all travel so much to so many exotic places. However, then, it was a treat for me to sit there and to listen to their experience and to dream about the day that I would travel to those places and have those experiences.

The Italian Mushroom Hunter

One of our neighbors enjoyed mushroom hunting when he lived in Italy. Like most Italians, he was also a great story teller.

He asked me one day, "What is the difference between a non-Italian Mushroom hunter and an Italian Mushroom Hunter?" When I told him that I did not know, he replied that "an Italian mushroom hunter will take the entire family to hunt for crimini, porcini, chanterelle mushrooms while a non-Italian goes alone" He told me of the passion that the people in Italy have for mushrooms and how the passion rises almost exponentially in one's pursuit for truffles, musty and intensely flavored. He told me how they used trained pigs to sniff out the mushrooms and how a good pig is worth its weight in gold to a farmer for the amount of quality mushrooms he can find.

However, I understand that they have now replaced the pigs with dogs that are now trained to unearth these treasures. The truffle-hunting dogs, generally mixed-breed mutts, can be worth $10,000 or more because of their skills. He also told me that much truffle-hunting is done under cover of darkness. I am told that the dogs, trained for three years and don't even do the digging once they catch the scent of their buried treasure. That task is left to the hunter, who digs into the side of a hill or toward the tree roots where the dog has found the mushroom scent. Most often the tree is oak, though it could be a willow, hazelnut or poplar.

Wise Neighborly Advice?

One of our neighbors was a little Old Italian lady who kept a magnificent garden despite the fact that she lived in a small row home with a small plot of land.

She will tell you that compost heaps can heat up to 140°F and 160°F. At that heat, disease organisms and the seeds from added weeds are destroyed. She used a garden hoe or rake to rotate the contents of the compost every other day, to make sure the leaves from the outside of the pile were moved toward the center. Within three months her compost was ready to be spread throughout her garden. She would always tell me that "it is important to provide the same nurturing to your children that you provide to your garden or you will not get good results"

It sounds like good advice to me.

EXAMPLES OF HISTORICAL FAMILY BUSINESSES

In the early days, Italian immigrants usually possessed two items, which had significant monetary value—their home and their business. It was there practice to past down these assets from generation to generation. Since both of these assets were very geographically stable, it is no wonder that the families stayed together in the same location for so many years since their livelihoods were so interdependent with their business.

The examples that we are about to present are cases in point. These are all family owned businesses in South Philadelphia that have been past on for generations. I am sure you can find examples in other "Little Italies" all over the United States.

Let's start by talking about the restaurant business since so many Italian-American families are in this business

THE ITALIAN-AMERICAN FAMILY RESTAURANT BUSINESS

A number of Italian-American families in South Philadelphia and many other communities are in the restaurant business. You will find some of the best Italian restaurants in the country there. Usually they are still preparing the dishes that their great-grandmother cooked for them when they were children.

Every Sunday, the sauce was cooking on a very old-school Italian stove. In many cases, mom and dad didn't even speak English, but their grandparents were in the restaurant cooking. They came from all sections of Italy and a variety of their home recipes were passed down from generation to generation. The head of the family that founded the restaurant usually worked two or three jobs to get enough money to start up in the restaurant business. The family business usually began as a pizzeria and expanded into serving other dishes from there. A few would expand by hiring a chef or engage a relative, usually the son, with an interest in baking and open a bakery in the lower level of the restaurant.

The restaurant was the perfect place for part-time jobs for the children after school. They would wait and bus the tables and deliver the pizzas. It was a great family activity. If you ask many of the Italian-American restaurant owners in the neighborhood they will tell you that their kids have been in the kitchen since they were babies.

Many of these owners are third generation. They inherited their business from their father who probably inherited from his father and have been doing this their whole life. They love the people that come into the restaurant and they treat their employees like their family.

The "Italian Godfather's" Dinner"

The greatest honor that an Italian-American restaurant owner can bestow on a customer is to give them an "Italian Godfather's Dinner" in their restaurant. The definition of this kind of dinner is (1) it is prepared personally by the owner of the restaurant (2) the chef decides on the menu for the guests and (3) it is at least a five course meal. The last time it was prepared for my guests and me was on my last trip to my hometown by Chef and Owner Mamma Maria of Mamma Maria's Restaurant in South Philadelphia. Chef Mamma Maria is a celebrity in Philadelphia. She owns a great Italian restaurant and has her own cooking show on WYBE TV in Philadelphia. She really knows how to cook a great Italian meal.

She treated Phyllis and I, my brother Bob and a group of my old fraternity brothers, to an authentic "Italian Godfather's Dinner". It was an elaborate six-course meal that she prepared herself. It blended the great traditions and taste that I remembered from my childhood. We arrived at the restaurant at 7 PM and we left at 1 AM. Momma spent most of the night at our table. We shared stories about our families and the traditions that we had in common.

Phyllis and I were leaving for our home in San Francisco the next morning but by the end of the night Momma was planning for our return trip to Philadelphia and told us what she was going to prepare for us the next time. This is another example of how the neighborhood considers itself one large family. I have not lived in South Philadelphia for 30 years but to Momma that did not matter. It was like I had never left.

Ralph's Restaurant

One great example of a family owned Italian restaurant is Ralph's in South Philadelphia. Ralph's Restaurant is a family owned business that has been in the Dispigno family for almost 100 years and still counting. Francesco Dispigno, an Italian immigrant who arrived from Italy in 1893 with his wife Catherine and their little boy Ralph had a vision that led him to a building at 901 Montrose Street in South Philadelphia, which he rented and opened his restaurant.

In 1905 their son Ralph, who was 15 at the time worked full-time in the restaurant. It was at that point that Francesco purchased the Montrose Street building. For the next decade the restaurant grew and prospered and in 1915 the Dispignos made a major decision to search South Philadelphia for a bigger place and found a boarding house that was built in the late 1800's as their new location. They used the bedrooms on the third floor of his new building as a small hotel and it served as the first home in the New World for several of his immigrant cooks and waiters. Francesco passed away in the early 1930's and Ralph was in charge of the day-to-day operation.

Ralph Dispigno Jr., Ralph's oldest son still makes his presence felt at the restaurant today.

Cannuli Bros. And Father

Cannuli's "House of Pork" is another 73-year-old legacy, passed from generation to generation. Dominic Cannuli in 1929, an immigrant from Italy, started the business. He opened a small butcher store in the "Italian Market" and sold quality meats for forty years. In 1969, Dominic's two sons, Anthony and Charles, took over the business and moved across the street to a larger property so that they could accommodate their customers. The business became "Cannuli Brothers" and their continued success led to additional growth.

In 1991, Charles Domenic Cannuli Jr. grandson of Dominic took ownership. They diversified the business and opened a poultry store connected to the "House of Pork". Today "Cannuli's House of Pork and Poultry" continues under his management.

Maggio Company

The Maggio Company is one of the early companies to arrive in the neighborhood. It was started by the four Maggio brothers in 1916 who were Sicilian immigrants. Their first cheese "factory" was located on a rented farm in Columbus, New Jersey. They operated their business there for several years and then relocated to Philadelphia.

Seven years and three moves later, the M. Maggio Company finally settled into its 9th and Montrose Streets location in South Philadelphia. By this time, only one brother, Michael was running the business. In 1998, the Maggio family sold their Italian Cheese business to Crowley Foods, Inc.

Termini Brother's Bakery

Another one of my fondest memories, especially around the holiday season, is visiting Termini Brother's Bakery. I must admit that I was introduced to Termini's by my wife, Phyllis, but it has been a tradition in her family since she was a little girl. Termini have been a tradition in South Philadelphia since the 1920's and a visit to Termini Brothers' Pastry offers immersion in a familiar and welcoming Italianate atmosphere.

Our relatives go there for many of the holidays to buy zeppoli for St. Joseph's day, bone-shaped ossimorti for All Soul's, pastiere and braided egg breads for Easter, torrone and cassata siciliana for Christmas. They also make one of the best Italian Rum Cakes you have ever eaten. That is why we ordered it as our wedding cake from them.

Tony's Produce & Anthony's Coffee House

Almost one hundred years ago, the Anastasio Family sailed the Atlantic Ocean from Eastern Sicily to come to America. They landed in Philadelphia and began working at Ninth and Christian Streets in what would later become an Italian-American village known as the Italian Market. They used a pushcart to sell fresh fish as the first Anastasio family business in Philadelphia. Soon, they purchased a store and began selling fish to their neighbors.

In 1938, their youngest son, Tony, opened a produce store specializing in vegetables and produce. Tony's store quickly became popular in the area. For more than fifty years, Tony Anastasio & Sons Produce was the anchor of the Italian Market's north end. In 1984, Tony's son began to build a wholesale division that soon became the principle service of the family business. Still in existence, the business is operated by members of the Anastasio family.

After traveling the country of Italy in the late 1980's, Tony's grandson, Anthony, returned with the idea to bring some romance, character and culture and opened the Italian Cafe' on Ninth Street. In early 1995, Anthony re-opened his grandfather's original store at 903 South Ninth Street as Anthony's Italian Coffee House.

I wish my children could have experienced all of these times and met these people and heard these stories. Their lives would be so much richer for the experiences. Below is a letter that I came across in my research. I do not know who the author is but it has a very interesting point of view about how things have changed and how much our children are missing by not having access to some of the people and traditions that we knew and loved.

The Joy of Growing Up Italian

Author Unknown

I was well into adulthood before I realized that I was an American. Of course, I had been born in America and had lived here all of my life, but, somehow it never occurred to me that just being a citizen of the United States meant I was an American. Americans were people who ate peanut butter and jelly on mushy white bread that came out of plastic packages. Me? I was Italian.

For me...as I am sure for most second-generation Italian American children who grew up in the 40's or 50's there was a definite distinction drawn between US and THEM. We were Italians. Everybody else—the

Irish, German, Polish, Jewish—they were the "Med-I-cans". There was no animosity involved in that distinction, no prejudice, no hard feelings, just—well—we were sure ours was the better way. For instance, we had a bread man; a coal and iceman, a fruit and vegetable man, a fish man and we even had a man who sharpened knives and scissors.

He came right to our homes or at least right outside our homes. They were the many peddlers who plied the Italian neighborhoods. We would wait for their call, their yell, and their individual distinctive sound. We knew them all and they knew us. Americans went to the stores for most of their foods, what a waste.

Truly, I pitied their loss. They never knew the pleasure of waking up every morning to find a hot, crisp loaf of Italian bread waiting behind the screen door. And instead of being able to climb up on the back of a peddler's truck a couple of times a week just to hitch a ride, most of my "Med-I-can" friends had to be satisfied going to the A&P. When it came to food, it always amazed me that my American friends or classmates only ate turkey on Thanksgiving or Christmas. Or rather, that they ONLY ate turkey, stuffing, mashed potatoes and cranberry sauce.

Now we Italians—we also had turkey, stuffing, mashed potatoes and cranberry sauce, but only after we had finished the antipasto, soup, lasagna, meatballs, salad and whatever else Mama thought might be appropriate for that particular holiday. This turkey was usually accompanied by a roast of some kind (just in case somebody walked in who didn't like turkey) and was followed by an assortment of fruits, nuts, pastries, cakes and of course, homemade cookies. No holiday was complete without some home baking; none of that store bought stuff for us. This is where you learned to eat a seven-course meal between noon and 4 p.m., how to handle hot chestnuts and put tangerine wedges in red wine. I truly believe Italians live a romance with food.

Speaking of food—Sunday was truly the big day of the week! That was the day you'd wake up to the smell of garlic and onions frying in olive oil. As you lay in bed, you could hear the hiss as tomatoes were dropped into a pan. Sunday we always had gravy (the Med-I-cans called it SAUCE) and macaroni (they called it PASTA). Sunday would not be Sunday without going to Mass. Of course, you couldn't eat before mass because you had to fast before receiving communion. But the good part was we knew when we got home we'd find hot meatballs frying and nothing tastes better than newly fried meatballs and crisp bread dipped into a pot of SAUCE.

There was another difference between US and THEM. We had gardens, not just flower gardens, but huge gardens where we grew tomatoes, tomatoes and more tomatoes. We ate them, cooked them and canned them. Of course, we also grew peppers, basil, parsley, lettuce and zucchini. Everybody had a grapevine and a fig tree and in the fall everyone made homemade wine, lots of it. Of course, those gardens thrived so because we also had something else it seemed our American friends didn't seem to have. We had a Grandfather!!

It's not that they didn't have grandfathers; it's just that they didn't live in the same house, or on the same block. They visited their grandfathers. We ate with ours and God forbid we didn't see him at least once per day. I can still remember my grandfather telling me about how he came to America as a young man, "on the boat". How the family lived in a rented tenement and took in boarders in order to help make ends meet. How he decided he didn't want his children, five sons and two daughters, to grow up in that environment. All of this, of course, in his version of Italian/English which I learned to understand quite well.

So when he saved enough, and I could never figure out how, he bought a house. That house served as the family headquarters for the next 40 years. I remember how he hated to leave, would rather sit on the back porch and watch his garden grow and when he did leave foe some special occasion, had to return as quickly as possible.

After all, "nobody's watching the house". I also remember the holidays when all the relatives would gather ay my grandfather's house and there would be tables of food and homemade wine music. Women were in the kitchen, men in the living room and kids, kids everywhere. I must have a half million cousins, first and second and some who aren't even related, but what did that matter.

And my grandfather, his pipe in his mouth and his fine moustache trimmed, would sit in the middle of it all grinning his mischievous smile, his eyes twinkling, surveying his domain, proud of his family and how well his children have done. One was a cop, one a fireman, one had his trade and of course there was always the rogue. And the girls, they had all married well and had fine husbands and healthy children and everyone knew respect.

He had achieved his goals in coming to America and to New York and now his children and their children was achieving the same goals that were available to them in this great country because they were Americans. When my grandfather died years ago at the age of 76 things began to change. Slowly at first, but then uncles and aunts eventually began to cut down on their visits.

Family gatherings were fewer and something seemed to be missing, although when we did get together, usually at my mother's house now, I always had the feeling he was there somehow. It was understandable of course. Everyone now had families of their own and grandchildren of their own. Today they visit once or twice a year.

Today we meet at weddings and wakes. Lots of other things have changed too. The old house my grandfather bought is now covered with aluminum siding, although my uncle still lives there and of course my grandfather's garden is gone.

The last of the homemade wine has long since been drunk and nobody covers the fig tree in the fall anymore. For a while we would make the rounds on the holidays, visiting family. Now we occasionally visit the cemetery. A lot of them are there, grandparents, uncles, aunts, even my own father.

The holidays have changed too. The great quantity of food we once consumed without any ill effects is no good for us anymore. There was too much starch, to much cholesterol, too many calories. And nobody bothers to bake anymore—too busy—it's easier to buy it now and too much is no good for you. We meet at my house now, at least my families do, but it's not the same.

The difference between US and THEM isn't so easily defined anymore, and I guess that's good. My grandparents were Italian Italians, my parents were Italian Americans, I'm American Italian and my children are American Americans.

Oh I'm an American alright and proud of it. Just as my grandfather would want be to be. We are all Americans now—the Irish, Germans,

Poles and Jews. U.S. citizens all—but somehow I still feel a little Italian. Call it culture, call it tradition, call it roots, I'm really not sure what it is. All I do know is that my children have been cheated out of a wonderful piece of their heritage. They never knew my grandfather.

10

The Value of a Strong Work Ethic

One of the values that the Italian immigrants brought to the United States was a strong work ethic and the desire to use that work ethic to achieve their dreams in the New World. Our parent's goal was that their children will be able to live a better life then they lived. And they were willing to work as hard as necessary to make that happen. Each generation of Italian-American standard of living rose a little higher through this attention to this work ethic. I remember my mother telling me, "Work hard enough and you will have what you want." But she also warned, "You will have nothing without working for it."

In this section, we will discuss some examples of Italian-Americans who though their strong work ethic achieved their goals in life. These are only some examples of the millions of Italian-Americans in the United States who have similar stories. I am using these as examples to demonstrate the strong sense on work ethic in the Italian-American community.

You will see that a number of the stories involve situations were this value was needed in the context of "never giving up" despite the odds. Life was desperate and hard or things were not going well and the person had to use the strength to work their way through the rough times. In other stories, you will see the individual using the strength to follow through on their dreams. They knew what they wanted and they would not be deterred, regardless of the hopelessness of the situation, until they achieved it.

Nicola & Lee Iacocco

A good example of this was the Iacocco family. Nicola Iacocco, father of Lee (famous for being CEO of Chrysler Corporation), came to the United States from San Marco in 1902 at age 12. He did odd jobs until he saved enough money to return to Italy in 1921 and bring his widowed mother back to the United States. While he was back in Italy, he fell in love with Antoinette who was 17 years old. They were married there and he brought both his mother and his new bride back to the United States.

Upon his return to the United States, Nicola opened a hot dog stand called Orpheum Wiener House, sold real estate, and started the first rental car business called U-Drive-It. All were successful despite the fact that he only had a 4th grade education. His son, Lido (Lee) Iacocco was born on October 25, 1924 to these Italian immigrants Nicola and Antoinette.

Lee is another good example of how strong work ethic and determination will help you succeed. Lee's first job was at the age of ten. He would take his wagon to the grocery store and wait for customers to leave the store and he would offer to pull their groceries home in return for a tip. When Lee turned 16, he worked 16 hours a day in a fruit market. He attributes his work ethic to the example set by his father.

After graduating from Leigh University, Lee landed a job at Ford but it was put on hold because he won the Wallace Memorial fellowship at Princeton. He graduated from Princeton and started working for Ford in 1946. He changed his name from Lido to Lee after going to work at Ford. He felt that it would be easier for business associates and contacts to recognize and understand him as Lee. When he took control over ailing Chrysler Corporation, he led by example. He reduced his annual salary to $1.00. When he paid back their government loan he commented: "We at Chrysler borrow the old fashion way. We pay it back." His family was very important to him throughout his career. One of his rules was to keep Friday night, Saturday, and Sunday for the family.

I can also attest to the Italian-American work ethic value in my own life. Throughout my childhood, the importance of working hard and paying my own way was stressed by my parents and all the other authority figures in my South Philadelphia community. It was "a badge of honor" in my neighborhood to have a job as a teenager. I had my first job at age nine. My father "suggested" to me that I should ask the grocer on the corner if he needed any help. It was a small, part-time, job stocking shelves in the corner grocery store but it meant a lot to me. I was "contributing" to my family's expenses, and I was an active "working" member of the community. It was a very rewarding experience for a young person.

I was not alone either. Most of the children in the neighborhood had part-time jobs at that time. It was expected by the fathers in the neighborhood that by the time you were a teenager, you were to start contributing to the household expenses. The by-product was that you were also learning to be independent and develop your own strong work ethic at an early age.

From the moment I accepted that first job at the grocery store, my father expected that I would not quit that job unless I had another job to replace it. Once I began working, you did not go back. From there, the "bar' was only raised higher. By the time I went to college, I had two jobs so that I could afford to pay my share of home expenses plus the increase expenses associated with college.

I attended LaSalle University, a private Catholic University in Philadelphia, which was very expensive. To afford the tuition, I worked 7 hours a night, three nights a week and Saturdays, at the Philadelphia Federal Reserve Bank in their Information Technology Department. On Saturday nights, I would work at the Philadelphia Bulletin, the local newspaper, to help distribute the Sunday morning edition. This plus a summer job and loans gave me enough money to finance my college education and contribute to family expenses.

This lesson of hard work has stayed with me until this day. I do not believe that I will ever retire. For better or worse, thanks to my father, I cannot see relaxing and not making money as a way of life.

Vince Lombardi

There are many other examples were the Italian-American "neighborhoods" had grown exceptional people with great work ethic. Take Vince Lombardi for example. Vince Lombardi is one of the most successful, admired and respected coaches in the National Football League. Vince was born in Brooklyn, New York on June

11, 1913. He was the first of five children. He was raised a Catholic and he studied for the priesthood for two years.

He started his football career as the star fullback for the St. Francis Preparatory High School football team. Vince was accepted to New York City's Fordham University in 1933 where he was a guard. He graduated cum laude with a business major in 1937. Over the next two years, Vince works at a finance company, took night classes at Fordham's law school, and played semi-pro football with Delaware's Wilmington Clippers. In 1939, he took a job at St. Cecilia High School in Englewood, New Jersey but left in 1947. In 1940, he married Marie Planitz and had a son, Vince Jr. and a daughter, Susan.

His dream was to coach football at a more competitive level. Between 1947 and 1958, Vince had a number of assistant coaching jobs at Fordham University; the United States Military Academy, and the New York Giants. By 1958, the 45-year-old coach wanted to a head coach. He accepted the job of leading the perpetual losers of the NFL: the Green Bay Packers.

Three years later, on December 31, 1961, Vince watched proudly as the Packers defeated the New York Giants 37-0 for the National Football League Championship. Under his leadership, the Packers dominated the league. In nine seasons they collected six division titles, five NFL championships, two Super Bowls, and a record of 98-30-4.

Vince was diagnosed with intestinal cancer and died on September 3, 1970. Over 3,500 people attended his funeral and Vince was buried in Mount Olivett Cemetery, in Middletown, New Jersey. Vince was inducted into the Professional Football Hall of Fame in 1971. That same year the Super Bowl trophy was renamed the *Vince Lombardi Super Bowl Trophy*.

◆   ◆   ◆

Growing up in South Philadelphia, Vince Lombardi was a real hero in our South Philadelphia neighborhood. When I was a 6th grader on the Saint Gabriel's Parish School's football team, I was using the uniform of an injured 8th grader who made sure that I knew that he wanted the uniform back when he recovered from his injury. The 8th grader would watch each practice while he was injured and catch me after practice and tell me to take care of his gear.

After two weeks of practice, he pulled me aside and told me that I wasn't a very good football player but I had the heart of Vince Lombardi. I took it as a compliment.

Antonetta & Geraldine Ferraro

In some cases, you have to dig deep down inside yourself and work even harder because of some difficult circumstances in your life. Take Antonetta & Geraldine Ferraro for example. Antonetta Ferraro is the mother of Geraldine Ferraro who is famous for being the first women nominated as Vice President of the United States by a major political party.

Antonetta's husband, Dominick Ferraro, an Italian immigrant, died when Geraldine was eight years old. Antonetta moved to the Bronx with her children where she found work sewing beads on wedding dresses and gowns to support her family. Despite all the hardships, she raised the children, including Geraldine. From those difficult circumstances, she reared a family, which included a woman who was considered for one of the highest elected post in the country. This can happen only in the United States.

Geraldine success also should not go unnoticed. She was born in Newburgh, New York in 1935. As Antonetta and Dominick's youngest child and only daughter, she over came the difficult circumstances of her father's death and the family's economic situation to receive a formal education at a Catholic school for girls and a scholarship to Marymount Manhattan College where she graduated in 1956.

She was a legal secretary for a period of time and then taught elementary school in Queens while attending Fordham Law School where she graduated in 1960. During the 1960s, Ferraro raised three children and practiced law occasionally at her husband's real estate office. In 1974, she headed a bureau of the district attorney office in Queens that dealt with child abuse, sex crimes, and crimes against the elderly. Ferraro sought the Democratic nomination for Congress for her district in 1978 and won reelection in 1980 and 1982.

At the Democratic National Convention in July, 1984, presidential nominee Walter Mondale selected Ferraro as his running mate. She then became the first women vice presidential nominee of a major party.

Dante Benedetti

Dante Benedetti is over 90 years old. He was born and raised in North Beach, the Italian neighborhood in San Francisco, California and has lived there his entire life. He managed the restaurant with his father where together they made wine, sausages and homemade prosciutto. Dante remembered his mom as a strong role model when he was growing up. He says that his mom was a tough little lady, and that she always wore wooden shoes.

He remembers if she gave him an order that he didn't like, she'd kick off her shoe from across the room and it would hit him in the chest. He would say, "But I didn't say anything," and she would say, "That was for what you were thinking." In those days it was simple, if you didn't follow the rules, you had to pay the price, but because of that, you developed a strong sense of character. When you get in trouble, it falls back on your family; you have to watch your step so you don't offend your family or your neighborhood.

His Dad opened his restaurant in 1918, and he followed his ways, and took it over when his dad died in 1951. He only recently sold the restaurant to a friend who owns another Italian restaurant down the street. He says that the new owner is a good man and he is happy. He allows Dante to still come into the restaurant every day and keep himself busy. It's still tradition that Dante's family always gets together for the holidays. His older daughter always has Easter and Thanksgiving at her home and his brother has them all over for Christmas every year—all 50 of them. One of the most important things Dante has learned is not to be an individual. He believes that you are one part of many. The emotional attitude you develop within a large family and community teaches you how to act in society.

Mary Lou Retton

Another example of work ethic has to do with the individual's completing a committed task regardless of the odds.

The story that I like to tell to emphasis this point and the determination and willingness to do whatever it takes to meet her life long goal is the story of Mary Lou Retton and the 1984 Olympics. In 1984, Mary Lou Retton was the first American women to win a gold medal in any event and the first American, male or female, to win the all-around.

Mary Lou Retton was born on January 24, 1968 in West Virginia as Mary Lou Rettoni. She wanted to be a gymnast since she was 8 years old. When she was 14, Mary Lou competed in meets throughout the world. She was coached by Bela Karolyi, the world famous gymnastic coach, who was impressed with her "hard to replace personality". Mary Lou Retton finished first in the 1984 Olympic trials. In 1984, at fifteen years-of-age, Mary Lou captured five medals in 1984 making her the star of the Games in Los Angeles.

However, she almost never attended those games. Prior to the Olympics she pushed herself very hard and just six weeks before the start of the games she had broken a cartilage in her knee off and the joints in her knee were locked up. She had to have an operation, and the doctors told her that she could not compete in the Olympics. Mary Lou responded, "I've made it this far—no one's going to keep me from trying. In three weeks she accomplished rehabilitation that would have normally taken three months to accomplish. If she had listened to the doctors, she would never have won the gold medal.

Mario Puzo

You can even be born in one of the most crime-ridden neighborhoods in the United States and, with determination; you can raise yourself out of that neighborhood and succeed with the right work ethic and the right motivation to succeed.

A good example of this is Mario Puzo. Puzo is one of America's most famous novelists. His best known novel is the *Godfather*. Mario Puzo, author of the bestseller "The Godfather" which spawned the Mafia film trilogy. Puzo won Oscars for screenplays for "The Godfather" and "The Godfather Part II." Puzo wrote several other novels about organized crime families, including "The Sicilian" and "The Last Don".

He was born in 1920 in the tough New York neighborhood of Hell's Kitchen on Manhattan's West Side. His parents were illiterate Italian immigrants. He served in Germany during World War II and attended New York's City College on the G.I. bill. He started writing pulp stories for "Male" and other men's magazines and published his first novel in 1955, "The Dark Arena," to enthusiastic reviews. His second book, "The Fortunate Pilgrim" was written in 1964, which Puzo took nine years to write, was an autobiographical family novel about Italian immigrants and brought Puzo some of his strongest reviews. Puzo said it was his best book but it did not bring him a lot of money.

Mario died on July 2, 1999 at his home in Long island. His novel *Omerta* was released a year later. In the fall of 2001, his final novel, *The Family*, was published.

John Ciardi

Sometimes, you can be surprised at what the skills and interest of the children that grows up in the Italian neighborhoods.

On such example is John Ciardi, the millionaire poet was born an immigrant's son in Boston's "Little Italy" in 1916. By 1986, he had built a reputation as a larger then life cultural legend. When poet John Ciardi died unexpectedly on Easter Sunday 1986, every major news outlet in the United States carried the news story. Ciardi had earned a reputation as a leading American literary figure. He was nationally known for his poetry. He published 21 volumes beginning in 1940 with four being published after his death. The last was published in 1997. He also brought poetry to the American people. In 1961-62, he had a network television program on CBS called *Accent* and his National Public Radio program called *A Word in your Ear* ran from 1977 to 1986.

He also had a twice a week magazine column called *Manner of Speaking* in the nationally known Saturday Review from 1961 to 1972. He was the first poet to have his own television and radio show. All this is what earned him his million dollar fortune. Cardi was a master at what he called the Unimportant Poem, the sort of poem written to celebrate nothing more then the sipping of coffee at breakfast or watching birds in the backyard. I guess he was the Jerry Seinfeld of that time.

Cardi wrote often about his Italian background. Italian Sunday dinners, favorite uncles and aunts, and his father' love for the opera. Cardi was so important to the literary landscape that he made two appearances to the Tonight Show with Johnny Carson.

Bonnie Tiburzi

Sometimes your hard work and devotion to achieve your goal makes you the first person to do so. That is what happened to Bonnie Tiburzi.

Bonnie Tiburzi is the first female pilot in commercial aviation history to fly for a major carrier when American Airlines hired her on March 30, 1973. She was also the first woman to earn her Flight Engineer's rating. Bonnie was born into an aviation family. Her father was a pilot during World War II with the Air Transport Company of TWA. By the age of twenty, she was flying copilot for a charter company in Europe. Another one of her first jobs was with a small commuter company in Florida flying DC-3s. They specialized in charter flights for sport fishermen. Bonnie reminds young women who dream of flying, "If you are determined, confident, and committed, you'll do fine. You have to be good."

Tiburzi has received several aviation awards including the Amelia Earhart Award in 1980 and the Outstanding Italian-American of the Year in 1974.

Frank Capra

Another Italian-American who was devoted to his craft and became a success was Frank Capra.

Frank Capra was born in Palermo, Sicily on May 19, 1897 but he emigrated the United States with his parents when he was six years old. They settled in Los Angeles where an older brother lived. From an early age, Frank proved to be a very ambitious person. He started by selling newspapers and worked his way through college and graduated in 1918 with a degree in chemical engineering.

He joined the Army in World War I and taught math to artillery officers. After the war, he began making short films in San Francisco in 1922 and became an editor and gag writer for Bob Eddy before moving to Hollywood to work for Hal Roach and Mark Sennett. Frank Capra was one of Hollywood's most gifted filmmakers. Some of his most recognized films include: *It Happened One Night*,

Mr. Deeds Goes to Town; *Lost Horizon*; *You Can't Take It With You*; and *Mr. Smith Goes to Washington*. He married Lucille Reyburn in 1932. Frank stopped making Hollywood films in the 1950s and devoted his talent to a science series for television and writing his autobiography *The Name Above The Title* in 1971.

During the dark decade of the 1930s, Frank Capra's films brought light where there was darkness and hope where there was despair. The Italian American director emigrated here from Sicily during the great migration As an immigrant himself, who celebrated his 6th birthday while in steerage aboard a ship bound for America, Capra felt a strong kinship for the suppressed and many of his characters symbolized the prejudice that awaited him in his new country.

Frank Capra's Christmas classic, it's a Wonderful Life (1946) is one of these enduring films. At the end of the film someone bumps the Christmas tree and a bell shakes and rings and little ZuZu say, "Look Daddy! Teacher says, Every time a bell rings, an angel gets his wings." We grew up with ZuZu each Christmas.

In 1982, he was awarded the American Film Institute's Life Achievement Award. Lucille died in 1984 and Frank suffered a stroke and remained in poor health until his death on September 3, 1991.

Yogi Berra

Yogi Berra is proof that you can work hard and have fun at the same time. Throughout his career, he has been known as a top-notch baseball player but he also has the reputation for being one of the "funniest ball players ever to play in the league". Lawrence "Yogi" Berra was born on May 12, 1925 in St. Louis, Mo. He grew up on Elizabeth Street in a neighborhood called "The Hill". As a boy, Yogi worked on a Coca Cola truck, pulled tracks in a train station, and shoveled coal to earn money for his family.

Yogi got his name from a childhood friend. While watching a movie about an Indian snake charmer, his friend noted that Yogi had a resemblance to the Hindu man, saying "That yogi walks like Lawdie (Larry) Berra," and the name stuck. Yogi joined the Navy when he was eighteen and he participated in the D-Day invasion at Omaha Beach, served in North Africa, and was also stationed in the States.

He began his career with the Yankees in 1946 as a platoon catcher. He received a $500 bonus to sign with the New York Yankees. Yogi was a fifteen-time All Star, winning the AL Most Valuable Player Award three times in 1951, 1954, and 1955. He played in 14 World Series and holds numerous World Series records including most games by a catcher (65), hits (71), and times on a winning team (10).

Yogi is one of the most quoted personalities of our time. Yogi's sayings seem to be all around us. Many times we hear the term "Yogi-isms"

"It ain't over till it's over"
"I really didn't say everything I said"
"You can observe a lot by watching"
"Never answer an anonymous letter"

Yogi was elected to the National Baseball Hall of Fame in 1972.

Antonin Scalia

Antonin Scalia was born in Trenton, New Jersey on March 11, 1936 from a Sicilian immigrant father and Italian-American mother. He received his BA from Georgetown University in 1957, and his law degree from Harvard University in 1960 and spent many years in private practice. President Reagan nominated Scalia to the US Court of Appeals for the District of Columbia in 1982. Four years later, Reagan nominated him to the US Supreme Court, and he took the oath of office on September 26, 1986.

Joe DiMaggio

Joseph Paul DiMaggio was born in Martinez, California on November 25, 1914. He was one of nine children born to Italian immigrants. He was signed as a shortstop by the San Francisco Seals at the age of 17. When Joe DiMaggio was growing up in California, his family not only taught him the value of hard work but also perseverance. Throughout his career, he was plagued by injuries that would have sidelined other players with less determination but he not only played but also excelled.

In 1933, his first minor league season, he hit in 61 consecutive games for the Seals. However, DiMaggio suffered a knee injury in 1934 and while this worried most of the other Major league teams at the time, the New York Yankees believed in him and signed him. He arrived in the major leagues with the Yankees in the spring of 1936. The "Yankee Clipper's" most famous record came in 1941 when he hit safely in 56 consecutive games. He left the Yankees to serve in the Army from 1943 to 1945. After 13 years with the Yankees and a career plagued with a long list of injuries, he called it quits in 1951. However, in that time, the Yankees won 10 American League Pennants and 10 World Series Championships. Joe DiMaggio received awards in 1939, 1941, and 1947 for the Most Valuable Player. He was also selected to the American League's All-Star team in each of the thirteen seasons he played in the major leagues.

All of these Italian-Americans have one thing in common. They were taught the value of hard work. They applied their determination to their desire to succeed and they accomplished their goals.

It is a lesson for us all.

11

The Value of Faith in God and Practice in Everyday Life

Our grandparents were generally very religious people. I cannot remember ever missing mass on Sunday during my 21 years in South Philadelphia. Rain or snow, we were in that pew on Sunday morning with the rest of the congregation listening to the priest giving the sermon of the week. Many of the older women in the neighborhood would go to mass every morning. It would not be unusual to see the early mass full with older Italian women praying for their families and their deceased relatives. After the mass, they would usually light a candle by the altar as a special request for some spiritual assistance.

In addition to these activities, there were a number of other activities in the neighborhood that demonstrated the extraordinary devotion the Italian–American community had toward God and the dedication that they showed to the Catholic Church. Many of these activities centered on the local parish.

Other times this devotion was shown in festivals that they held in the neighborhood. These festivals were elaborate affairs were everyone participated and were fun as well as demonstrated devotion to God and the Saints that they were honoring. Another way to show this devotion to God was for the individual to commit his/her life to the service of God by joining a religious order. Many Italian-American families had a brother or sister, aunt or uncle in a religious order in the Catholic Church.

In this section, we will discuss each of these areas and give examples of Italian-American people or institutions that did just that. Let's begin with the activities of the local parish.

THE ITALIAN-AMERICAN CATHOLIC PARISH

Despite the fact that these parishes were small, approximately 100 families each, it would not be unusual for each parish to have <u>forty-five active organizations</u> where parishioners of all ages could volunteer to support the parish's activities and the needy in their community. The parishioners were very active in their church and community. Some of the organizations within the average parish are described below as examples.

The Pastoral Council would be a consultative body with whom the Pastor could reflect with and ask for assistance to guide the overall care and ministry of the Parish. Our parish council was very active and was very involved with the pastor and the families in the parish.

The Stewardship Committee would promote Stewardship as a Way of Life within all aspects of the Parish community. It would be responsible for implementing the gift-based ministry and discipleship of the parish. They would oversee special campaigns, such as the Annual Catholic Charities Appeal and discerning a portion of the parish's funds for the poor and others in the community. My mother participated in the activities of this committee at St Gabriel. As you would expect, fund raising was a major part of their responsibility.

The Parish would have Sunday school programs for children, usually ages three through kindergarten, each Sunday. The children would be involved in many of the services of the parish in one form or another. They usually had a singing role too.

There would be a Bereavement Team that provides a connection between the parish and the family of the departed. Members of this Ministry would visit the families and offer assistance in planning the funeral Mass. Members would also preside at the prayer service at the funeral home and still other members would pray for the deceased and their families. This committee was very personal and it was not unusual that they would organize the neighbors to assist the family of the departed even after the funeral.

The Care Ministry would be a group of volunteers which provided transportation to doctor and hospital appointments, blood tests, etc. for the people of the parish in need a ride or other assistance. I also remember this group helping many families who were in trouble because the father had lost his job or someone in the family had become temporary ill and needed a little extra hand. Feed the needy team members provided a meal to the less fortunate of the community. Meals were prepared and served at the Church.

Other volunteer groups in this small parish would include ushers, scripture studies, Knights of Columbus, altar boys, church cleaners, woman group, a youth ministry, host families, church choir, newsletter staff, retreat committee, sacristans and many more.

This small Catholic Parish would be only one of the 24 parishes in South Philadelphia with all of these actively supported by the parishioners of all ages to assist the community in many areas of need. This is another example of Italian-American values in action.

<u>Parish Student Chores</u>

Another one of the parental duties exercised by the parish was to provide you with activities to keep you busy during your non-school time. The Catholic Church knew better then anyone that "idle hands were the devils workshop". They organized a number of activities or assignments that were heavily attended by the students. Student chores were assigned by the priests and nuns to most of the students at the beginning of each semester and were expected to be accomplished as part of your course work and tuition payment to the parish.

These chores would include a variety of assignments including cleaning up the classroom after class; janitorial services; gardening & snow removal; church, rectory, & nunnery clean-up services; etc. These chores were done after class and considered part of our tuition and helped in the upkeep of the parish property. In our early years, the chores were less stressful. I remember in the early grades, my jobs included such chores as erasing and cleaning the blackboards; sweeping the classroom floors; and emptying the wastepaper baskets.

As we grew older, the jobs were harder and the responsibilities grew as well. The middle grades saw me move to some yard work where I received an appreciation of how to mow a lawn and care for plants. By the time I was in the higher grades, I was doing some office work assisting in the rectory. It also gave each of us an appreciation of the work necessary to keep the parish maintained; and we also got to know the priest and nuns a lot better. We never thought of defacing or "trashing" the property because we knew that we would be the ones who would have to clean it up. Can you imagine the outcry from the public if students were given "chores" today in school?

Parish School Safety Patrol

Another parish student organization was the safety patrol. It was composed of students of the 6th to 8th grades. They were positioned on street corners, within two blocks of school, one hour before and after the school bell rang. Their job was to monitor traffic and cross the small children (grades 1 through 5) to assure they would cross the street safely. This group was another example of how the child was taught responsibility at an early age and they also provided a legitimate function because they helped the younger children cross the street in safety.

Parish School Raffles

Each week the parish would have a raffle. The grand prize would be $ 1,000. Each student would be responsible for selling $10.00 worth of raffle tickets each week. The drawing was held every Saturday in the parish gymnasium and it was a big affair. The proceeds would go to the parish to pay for your tuition (either in the parish school or high school).

The only other gambling competition in South Philadelphia at the time was "the numbers" and "bingo". The "numbers" were illegal and I think it was run by the mob. Bingo was also run by the parish. The "numbers" was an illegal underground betting game in South Philadelphia that you could play each day. You would bet money on three numbers and you would get odds if those numbers came out. I remember the various ways that the people used to pick the numbers including magic spells, dreaming, superstitions etc.

When you saw someone in the neighborhood with a new major appliance or a new car, the natural reaction was: "They must have hit the numbers or won the Parish raffle".

The Italian-American Funeral

I was an altar boy at St. Gabriel's parish. In addition to assisting the priests at mass, one of my duties as an altar boy was to participate at Catholic Funeral services for the recently departed parishioners. One of the traditions that I remember vividly while living in South Philadelphia was how the Italian-American family paid such respect to a family member who died. As an alter boy at St. Gabriel's Parish School, I participated in numerous funerals and had a close up look at how a number of Italian-American ceremonies were actually conducted.

Despite the fact that many of these South Philadelphia families were poor, they would spend a great deal of money on these funerals for their loved ones. For example, they purchased the deceased person new clothes, the best casket, the most expensive burial plot and other amities.

A sociologist may tell you that these Italian families deprived themselves of its limited comforts and sacrificed any small reserve of cash that they might have because they were a "death oriented society." This "death oriented society" believed that their loved ones were just passing from one life to another and never really leaving the family so they were compelled to make sure that they had all they need to be able to find their way and be comfortable in their new life.

My grandfather told me that the funeral ritual pattern used in South Philadelphia is modeled after the system of the "Signore". This ritual was used by the landowners in Italy for whom the peasants work before they immigrated to the United States. There are also a number of traditions that are part of the ritual. For example, at a number of funerals that I attended where I saw Italian women place cigarettes, lighters, money or other personal items in the casket near the body. I was told by my father that this is an Italian custom and it is done in order to calm the soul on its journey.

I have also seen situations where women have forgotten to put some personal items in the casket and they would place it in the casket of another person who died later in hopes that the two souls would meet later.

I have witnessed the tradition where the body was always carried out feet first. This was done in order that the soul would not be able to find its way back into the house if it returned. This was done because he would not see the door as the corpse left and therefore not be able to locate it again later.

When we would drive to the cemetery in the funeral procession, the car made frequent stops and turns to confuse the soul's sense of direction. The return to the house was always made by a different route. My grandfather told crying and lamenting which began at the time of the death was forbidden at the funeral because the soul might hear and lose its way.

My wife Phyllis attended her Grandfather Frank De Laurentis' funeral at
18 months old to show respect.

Mourning for the deceased did not end on the day of the funeral. The person was still part of your family and continued to be remembered and be active in family situations especially on Sunday when the family would meet at the cemetery and on the Day of the Dead.

Honoring the dead family members did not end with the funeral. . One example of remembering them was every November 2, The Day of the Dead, the family would go to mass, visit the grave, and leave the food for deceased on the dining table in case the soul returned that night.

Families also remembered their deceased relatives almost every Sunday. When I was young, I went with my friend and his whole family to the Cemetery one Sunday to visit their deceased grandfather. Their children and I played in the grass next to the grave and there was chatting and gossiping among the families who had plots nearby. His mother even planted flowers around the head stone of his grandfather and they had a picnic lunch around the grave. It may sound strange now but it was a loving sign that was intended to show respect for their departed loved grandfather and wanted to be with him on a bright sunny day.

Over time, the funeral was seen as the family's final expression of recognition for one of its members and ultimately became a stage for competition in our neighborhood. Each one became more lavish then the last.

The better the display, the higher the admiration was for the family. In some cases, the family would be criticized if their funeral were not grand enough. Individuals who spent less than expected were referred to as *sfaciade* (bad fronted, bad appearing).

Today, Italian-Americans in South Philadelphia place more emphasis on the way that the body is "laid out" at the funeral parlor. Funeral bands stopped escorting the body to the church about 1955 and the church outlawed tombstone pictures, very tall stones, and planting at the gravesites. My mother said that the reason for these changes told to her by undertakers was always "for uniformity"

While the emphasis upon the journey of the soul appears to have disappeared from the ritual, some signs still remain especially in the floral arrangements.

The specific floral forms used by many Italian-Americans in South Philadelphia today are those of the signori. At the wakes that I have attended, I have seen the floral forms of the "Gates of Heaven," the "Half Moon with Star," and the "Stopped Clock". These symbolize the concept of the journey concept.

My father told me that the "Gates" symbolize the soul getting through the gates to heaven, and that the "Crescent Moon and Star" are direction aids because the soul goes between the crescent and the star. He said that the hands of the "Clock" are stopped at the exact time that death is thought to have occurred. This also signifies the beginning of the journey of the soul to their new life.

Perhaps in the next generation the funeral symbols will finally disappear as new needs make changes in the lives of Philadelphia's Italians. But for now, it is a way to collectively express their sorrow and celebrate the life's achievements of a departed relative and to continue to remember them.

<u>Parish Altar Boys</u>

I also have other fond memories of my services as an altar boy in assisting the priests in the celebration of Mass and performing other Catholic ceremonies. If you "played your cards right", you could also make a part time job out of your service as an alter boy. The difficult part about becoming an altar boy in those days was learning Latin. All of the ceremonies, at that time, were celebrated in Latin so you were required to learn the language.

Another disadvantage was the uniform. Let's just say that it was not stylish. I remember taking a lot of ribbing from my buddies for wearing that "dress" during the various ceremonies. But there were some advantages too. One was the ability to get you out of class. You cannot imagine how many opportunities you had to leave class to conduct Mass; practice for various religious ceremonies; and work with the priest on various other projects. It was a gold mine!

Another benefit was that you were keeping busy serving Mass on Sunday with the priest rather then sitting idle in the pew with your family. I would prefer to be active on the altar rather then just sitting there and just watching. The people in the pews all looked so very bored.

The last benefit was that part-time job that I mentioned. In addition to the routine Mass, the altar boys would be called upon to assist in the parish's weddings and funerals. At each wedding and funeral, it was the parish tradition to pay the church a stipend.

It was also the custom for the family to give a "little something" (i.e. money) to the altar boys. The family would usually give each alter boy $5.00 or $10.00 each. This was a significant amount at the time and therefore it was a great benefit in a Parish where you could have a number of weddings and funerals in an average month.

For two years, I was the lead altar boy at the parish. In this role, I scheduled the altar boys, including assigning those alter boys to perform each wedding and funeral. As you can image, it made me a very popular person among the altar boys.

RELIGIOUS FESTIVAL TRADITIONS

Italian religious festival traditions are a great way to honor your religious beliefs and have fun as well. People come together in the neighborhood to honor God and the patron Saint as well as to share their history and the values, which unite them. For example, an Italian patron saint's day festival creates a community based on devotion. The neighborhood is cleaned up and decorated. The statues of saints in the church basement are dusted off and hung with ribbons.

On the Sunday nearest the saint's day, we would have a procession after Mass. The statues would be carried or pulled through the streets of the neighborhood, outlining the boundaries of the parish. During the ceremony they raise sacred symbols—cross, statues, and banners. They link the participants of the ceremony vertically to the divine. The statues are carried through the streets and they draw a circle around the neighborhood with the parish church. Each individual declared their allegiance by stepping behind the saint of their devotion.

Let's discuss a few examples. One example is a festival held each year by the Society of Saints Cosmas & Damian.

Society of Saints Cosmas & Damian

The Society of Saints Cosmas & Damian celebrates an annual festival to the Saints in Utica, New York that attracts thousands of people each year and is an excellent reminder of our heritage and many Italian-American Catholic values. Born in Cilicia, (now known as Arabia), in the third century, Cosmas and Damian were the first children born in a family of seven boys. The twins studied medicine and are credited for being the first to attempt a limb transplant on a human being.

They devoted themselves to rich and poor alike, accepting no payment for their medical services, thus earning their title, "The Silver-less Ones". These miraculous patrons of medicine were accused of being Christians by two fellow doctors and arrested by Lisia, the governor of the city of Aega. They were tried in a court of Ceasar and sentenced to death by torture.

Their first torture was being cast into the sea with both hands and feet bound. A miracle occurred as they became free, enabling them to swim ashore. Their second torture was burning at the stake. A second miracle occurred as the flames failed to burn them. The third torture was flogging. A third miracle occurred, as the whips would not hit their marks. After a final demand that they renounce their Christian faith was refused, Saints Cosmas & Damian were decapitated. The day was September 27 in the year 287.

Saints Cosmas & Damian are the patrons of the city of Gaeta, Italy. It is believed that through their intercession the city's population was spared during an 18th century plague.

The Society of Saints Cosmas & Damian is an Italian American organization made up of approximately 100 individuals. The Society was formed in 1926, during a period of heavy immigration to this country by many people of Europe.

A large group of immigrants from the beautiful coastal city of Gaeta, Italy, settled in Cambridge and Somerville, Massachusetts. Hungry to fit into their new surroundings, most of these people were eager to learn a new language and a new way of life, which would most certainly provide a better future for their children. Most worked in the local meat packing industry, a far reach from their native fishing or farming professions.

A sense of community belonging and cohesion was brought about in many ways for these people, but mainly through religion. A local Italian Roman Catholic Church was opened by the Archdiocese of Boston to service this group, but many longed for the traditions, which were left behind. They specifically wanted a religious festival. In response to this longing, a small group of women began to meet periodically to pray to the patron Saints of their beloved city of Gaeta, Saints Cosmas & Damian.

The group grew and started to meet monthly in larger facilities. Soon thereafter a group of men organized and sent to their homeland for life-sized images of their patron Saints. When the statues arrived, the organization began a yearly festival in honor of these beloved Saints. The year was 1926.

The celebration begins on Saturday evening when the statues of Saints Cosmas and Damian are taken out of their chapel. The statues are brought to the doorsteps as the American and the Italian National Anthems are played. Next, the band plays the, "Lind" or "Hymn", (the traditional song of Saints Cosmas & Damian), and the traditional, "Marcia Reale", as the saints are taken out of the building. Barrages of fireworks and confetti greet the statues as they are presented to the crowd of devotees. A candlelight procession then follows and the festival opens as the statues are swayed down the main street of the feast. The statues are then placed in a temporary outdoor chapel as a, "Healing Service", is conducted with the Relic of Saints Cosmas & Damian for all in attendance.

Music, food, carnival and games continue throughout the evening. At 11pm, the statues are taken back to their permanent chapel. The members of the society remain through the early hours of the morning, preparing for, "The big day".

Sunday morning, the chapel is opened at 8am. Coffee and Italian pastries are served for all who will march in the morning procession to church. The society women wear purple satin capes for this special procession. Many children will also walk to church. The statues are again taken out of the chapel in traditional fashion as the bands play. The church will fill to capacity for 9:30am Mass as parishioners, local guests, and visitors from all parts of the country come to see these beloved, "Healing Saints".

At the conclusion of the Mass, the procession returns to the chapel, Porter Street is closed, and the society hosts traditional, Italian, Sunday dinner for all.

At 1pm, the, "Grand Procession", begins. The society members, several bands, floats, and devotees, march as the statues of Saints Cosmas and Damian are carried through the streets of the surrounding neighborhoods of East Cambridge and Somerville. The procession will continue for many hours, as the route is filled with families hosting, "Open House", for friends and family. The statues are stopped and set down as crowds gather to gaze, and individuals approach these miraculous icons. Devotees will touch the Saints, and offer donations of money or golden mementos for favors received and continued good health and tranquility.

As the statues are set in front of the homes of these devoted families, they are greeted with fireworks, confetti, balloons, and ribbons, blankets, capes, or sashes filled with monetary donations.

Whenever the statues are stopped, the band plays the traditional hymn, followed by any requested favorites. As the statues are moved away, they are lifted in the air 3 times to signify blessing to the home and family. This ritual continues throughout the afternoon and into the evening as so many returns to stop the Saints in front of the homes they once lived in as well. The procession winds its way back to the festival area by 8pm, and entertainment for all ages continues until 10pm, when the statues are carried back to their permanent chapel.

The families involved in the festival work on preparations for weeks. For them, this event is of utmost importance.

In the 1940's, the women members, led by Marietta Colarutolo, purchased a parcel of land on Porter Street in East Cambridge and funded the building of a chapel for the statues.

The building would house the Saints and serve as a meeting place for monthly meetings. The feast became a major event in the lives of these founding members, as well as in the lives of their families. Over the years, much has changed. "The old neighborhood", has been transformed as the older generations pass on, and the young move to the suburbs. Religion and devotion, as we now know them, are a far fetch from what our grandparents knew, and backyard tomato gardens have been replaced with lush lawns.

The feast lives on in its original form however. The location of the festival itself has moved by a block or two, but the tradition, as it was intended, lives on in the hearts of the descendants of those who began the festival. The families all return to, "The old neighborhood", for this yearly reunion. The present members of this organization are evermore involved in organizing the feast, and they represent all ages. Many represent the 5th generation of membership for their families.

Most work tirelessly to carry on the tradition, and preserve the prominent presence of the Society in the local community. The Society is represented by various members' at all local happenings.

In 1988 the Smithsonian Institute asked the Society to recreate its festival on, "The Mall", which spans between our nation's Capitol Building, and the Washington Monument. The festival lasted 2 days and took place over the July 4th holiday. Over 3 million people were present for this spectacular celebration.

The chapel underwent a major renovation in 1995, and the men's and women's Societies have now joined to be known as one large organization, "The Society of Saints Cosmas & Damian of Cambridge and Somerville, Massachusetts". Membership is at an all time high.

Our Lady of Mount Carmel, Hammonton New Jersey

Another example of an organization that was formed to honor God and to do good works in his name is the Our Lady of Mount Carmel Society. The Our Lady of Mount Carmel Society is an independent nonprofit Catholic Organization formed in 1875 by Italian immigrants new to Hammonton, New Jersey, They took time to celebrate their safe journey to America and a successful harvest by giving praise and thanks to the Blessed Virgin Mary.

The main function of the Our Lady of Mt. Carmel Society is the preparation and presentation of the feast each July 16th. Phyllis's family would take her to this event each year. She would enjoy the excitement of the crowds, the Italian food, and the games. The Society is also involved in a variety of community activities and charitable endeavors, regularly supporting school, community and church fund raising efforts. From those beginnings, the Mt. Carmel Society has continued forward to this day. The Society consists of members of each of the town's three Catholic Church parishes and beyond. Since its inception, membership in the society has generally passed from father to son.

It all began in 1875 at the home of Antonio Capelli where they prayed in thanks for their safe journey to America, for a successful farming season, and for the blessings and good fortune found in their new home of Hammonton. From this beginning the Feast has gone on to become one of the longest continuous celebrations of its kind. Many of the faithful make an annual pilgrimage as an act of faith as thanks for their own blessings, or as an act of devotion to the Blessed Mother.

The Feast and the town grew very quickly. By 1886, the Feast was moved to the Hammonton Lake Park. St. Joseph Church—the first Catholic Church to be built in Hammonton, became a focal point for the celebration. In 1905, the Our Lady of Mount Carmel Society was chartered as an independent organization. It remains as such today, with its membership encompassing members of all three parish churches in Hammonton.

The Festival continues to this day, as always, centered around the procession on the Feast day of July 16th. Masses are held all day. St Joseph Church has a shrine to the Blessed Mother where the faithful have come to worship for over 50 years at the Festival.

Feast of St. Anthony of Padua, South Philadelphia

My family would attend this event annually and it would be one of the highlights of our year. The form of Italian-Saint's day processions has changed little since the period of Italian immigration. Every June 13th, in the early morning, you will hear firecrackers at 62nd and Grays Ferry Road to open the feast of St. Anthony of Padua.

A band will play the American and Italian anthems, as the flag bearers will come out, and proceed to the door of the president of the St. Anthony Society. The standard bearers of six other societies are then collected, and the procession begins. Statues of the saints, finishing with St. Anthony, are carried out of Our

Lady of Loreto Church and placed on carts. Little girls carry flowers or hold ribbons dangling from the statues. The faithful pin money on the statues.

As the procession passes each house, its inhabitants join the procession, following their favorite saint. Neighbors put out lemonade to ease people's thirst during the three-and-a-half hour march. Detours are made to the houses of the very old and the shops of merchants whose support of the festival has been especially generous. For the last block St. Anthony is lifted from his pedestal and carried,

Such religious festivals were the center of Southern Italian religious life. For the immigrant, whose loyalty was not to Italy but to the village of his birth, the festival became an important symbolic link. As more people from Italian villages immigrated to the United States a few families would form a society to procure a statue, solicit contributions from paesani for a band and fireworks, and recreate the procession in America. The reputation of the home village depended on a good turnout to these festivals and a strong sense of rivalry persisted even when the village ceased to be the unit of procession participants.

COMMITTING LIVES TO GOD

The two examples that I will use for people who have committed their lives to God are people who have similar backgrounds to my own. They are both Italian-Americans who were born in South Philadelphia and both graduated from Bishop Neumann High School. I am sure that, as with all my examples, these are just a few, of thousands of examples that can be used of Italian-Americans that could make my point.

Rev. Richard Antonucci, O. Praem

Richard Antonucci was born and raised in South Philadelphia to a family with strong Italian roots. All four of his grandparents were immigrants from Southern Italy and his grandmother, Lucia, lived with his family all through his childhood and high school years. He graduated from Bishop Neumann High School and decided to devote his life to God by joining the Norbertine Order of Priest.

Based on his writings, one priest in particular, Fr. George Feider took him under his wing and made him feel very special. He shared with him that he might like to join the Norbertine Order and become a teacher at Neumann. He saw the Norbertines as very different from the other priests in that they seemed to really enjoy being with one another. He stated in his writing how he will never forget how one priest, Fr. Fred Becker, his junior-year English teacher, would joke around with his conferes very openly. And, he remembers being surprised by that. It sounds strange now…. Being surprised at priests joking around with one another…. But back then it made a very positive impression on me. "Boy, it must be great being like that," he remembers thinking.

He spent most of his priesthood years in the educational ministry. As a high school math and computer teacher, He is now am the Development Director at Daylesford Abbey.

Rev. John Zagarella, O. Praem

John Zagarella also was born in South Philadelphia and attended grade school years at Epiphany of Our Lord parish. He said that he was intrigued early in his life about the lives of the priests and sisters that educated him there. By Christmas of Third Grade, He was receiving his education about things intellectual and spiritual under the guidance of the Sisters of Saint Joseph. Less than a year after his move into Catholic school, he was in training to serve as an altar boy.

In his mind, it is crystal clear that it was in the care of the Sisters and priests at that important time in his life, in conjunction with his parents that fostered respect for our faith that the stirrings of a vocation to the priesthood were like John, many of the Norbertines of Daylesford Abbey graduated from Bishop Neumann/Saint John Neumann High School in South Philadelphia.

By the time he had graduated from Neumann, he befriended a few of the Norbertines at school, and learned a little more about what their lives were like. He discovers that teaching was only a part of their priestly ministry. In addition there were the Sunday Masses, the weddings, funerals, ministering to the sick and dying, their guidance to young and old through various trials and tribulations of life. It was evident by the end of his senior year that he was going to enter the Norbertine Community. After high school, he entered Villanova University and was ordained a priest on June 21, 1986. His assignments have included both principal and president of Saint John Neumann High School. He presently resides at the Abbey.

God and the Catholic Church were a significant part of the Italian-American community and, to this day, still is in many families. However, the number of priest and nuns entering religious orders are down as is church attendance in many areas. But there is resurgence in interest in God and religion. I hope we see more interest in learning about these subjects from our children in the future.

12

The Value of Committing Yourself to Serving Others

Service to others is a deeply held value in the Italian-American community. If anyone in my family had only one dollar and you needed it, they would give it to you. The people in the neighborhood were very close. If someone needed anything, they were there to help. We will talk about some examples of this in this section of the book. These are only a few examples of thousands of Italian-Americans who have served others throughout the last hundred and fifty-five years since the great migration.

I have chosen them just to demonstrate the breath of commitment that individual Italian-Americans have toward service to their community. You will recognize some familiar names like A.P. Giannini, founder of the Bank of America and Fiorello LaGuardia, the famous mayor of New York City but you will also read stories of people who are not so easily recognizable such as Dominic Renzulli.

We will also discuss examples of Italian-American organizations that provide a number of valuable services within the community including UNICO, the Augustus Society, the NYPD Columbia Association, The Italian-American Brotherhood Club and others. But you will find many more if you look around your neighborhoods.

INDIVIDUALS

A.P. Giannini

A.P. Giannini is a man who felt deeply about his responsibility to others. He was a very wealthy man in more way then one. A.P. Giannini was the founder of the Bank of America. The Bank of America was the largest bank in the United States in the late 20th Century. A.P. was born in San Jose, California in 1870. He was born in a hotel managed by his 22-year-old father, Luigi, who was a recent immigrant from Italy. His mother was a 15-year-old woman named Virginia.

Luigi did well for the family economically and in 1869 they moved to a 40-acre parcel in the Santa Clara Valley. However, the American dream was soon to be a nightmare for A.P. An employee murdered Luigi, and Virginia, only 22-years-old at the time, and with three boys, had to carry on by herself. A few years later she married Lorenzo Scatena. In 1882, when A.P. was 12, the family moved to San Francisco. Lorenzo did well marketing produce. A.P. worked for him and soon he became a partner in his firm, Scatena's company.

In 1892, he married Clorinda Agnes Cuneo. Together, they invested wisely in real estate and by 1901 they were rich, but A.P. said: "I don't want to be rich. No man actually owns a fortune; it owns him". When A.P.'s father-in law died in 1902 he left a fortune, 11 children, and no will. A.P. took over the estate and managed it effectively. The assets included some shares in a bank: the Columbus Savings and Loan. A.P. was invited to sit on the Board. His experience on the Board of that bank was so bad that he decided to start a new bank in 1904, the Bank of Italy, for the purpose of helping the community. This bank ultimately became Bank of America, at one time, the largest bank in the United States.

A.P. is known for his creativity; innovation; sensitivity to his customers in banking industry. When the earthquake and subsequent fire destroyed much of San Francisco in 1906, the Bank of Italy survived and was one of the first banks to make funds available to the community. The bank also survived the national panic of 1907 because A.P. had the foresight to hoard gold when the impending signs of trouble loomed. A.P. also saw the merits of branch banking when so many others were terrified by the prospect. He bought banks throughout California and in 1927 consolidated them into the Bank of America of California. He introduced novel lending practices; created the BankAmericard, now know as Visa.

In1945, he gave half of his assets, $509,000, to the Bank of America-Giannini Foundation. He did not believe in amassing a great fortune. His net worth at his death in 1949 was $489,000.

The Giannini Family Foundation supports medical research fellowships and organizations engaged in research and education to improve the quality of life for people with hemophilia. The Fellowship program supports promising young investigators in the early stages of their postdoctoral training in medical research. Since 1951, the Ginannini Family Foundation has supported 414 fellows engaged in medical research at California's eight accredited medical schools.

Fiorello H. LaGuardia

Standing only a little over five feet tall Fiorello H. LaGuardia's impact on New York City far outweighed his physical presence. Beginning as a Congressman representing Greenwich Village, LaGuardia soon received a reputation for being a fiery speaker and an untiring advocate of his constituents. In his first bid for the City's top position he was defeated. However by the 1933 election, events in New York made his election on the "fusion" ticket a sure thing. Serving from 1934 to 1945 he was one of only three modern day mayors to serve 3 consecutive terms in office.

He guided the City thorough the turbulent and difficult period of the Great Depression and later oversaw the City's transformation into a vital component of The United States efforts in World War II. Propelled by boundless energy, LaGuardia initiated numerous reforms to combat urban poverty, rebuild decaying infrastructure, put thousand of New Yorkers back to work and laid the groundwork for what would become modern day New York.

LaGuardia was born on December 11, 1882, to Achille Lugi LaGuardia, an Italian immigrant, who would serve as a bandmaster in the US Army, and Irene Cohen a Jewish immigrant from Austria-Hungary. Although born in New York City LaGuardia grew up in the southwestern territories that would eventually become New Mexico and Arizona. LaGuardia then obtained a position with the

US Consular Service in 1901 where he served in Budapest, Trieste and Fiume, Hungary

In 1907 LaGuardia returned to New York. Here he worked at Ellis Island, the main port of entry into the United States as a translator. LaGuardia used his knowledge of five languages to help new immigrants in becoming US citizens. While at Ellis Island, LaGuardia was attending Law School at New York University. He graduated in 1910 and joined a law firm where he represented immigrants, the poor and workers.

He also was involved in Republican politics. In 1914 he ran for Congress in the heavily democratic neighborhood of Greenwich Village. He lost in his first bid but he ran a second time and was elected on November 7, 1916 to his first public office. LaGuardia remained in Congress until 1932, except for his service during World War I as a Pilot and a term as President of the city Board of Aldermen.

In Congress, LaGuardia had a reputation as a progressive leader. During the 1920's he was criticized for what he saw as unfair immigration restrictions. He opposed prohibition and fought for labor unions. In 1932 he co-sponsored the Norris-LaGuardia Act, which restricted Federal courts from issuing injunctions to stop union activities.

LaGuardia ran for Mayor of New York in 1933 pledging to clean up city government and break the stranglehold of the Tammany machine. When LaGuardia's coalition won, the new mayor went to work to take control of the city's government. He fought to take charge of the city's finances from the banks and balanced the budget. Within its first year the LaGuardia administration had built over 50 new playgrounds and planned 60 new parks, many in poor neighborhoods. Throughout his administration, slums were torn down and replaced with public housing and schools. Hospitals, Child and countless other social welfare centers were converted to Health Stations to improve the health and sanitary conditions of the City.

In 1946 he was appointed the Director General of the United Nations Relief and Rehabilitation Administration, providing food, clothing and shelter to millions of Europeans displaced by World War II. His efforts to rebuild Europe, however, were cut short when, despite his best efforts UNRRA was disbanded at the end of December, 1946. In 1947 he was diagnosed with pancreatic cancer. Almost until his final day he continued to speak about the direction he thought the City, the Nation and the World should be taking. On September 20, 1947 "The Little Flower" died. His funeral attracted thousands who came to say farewell.

LaGuardia's years as mayor marked the emergence of modern New York City. His spirit for action transformed a city made up of individual boroughs into a single city with one vision and a single purpose. He saw a vision of a modern city of tunnels, airports and bridges that must also have adequate housing, schools and playgrounds.

G.Fred DiBona

G. Fred DiBona Jr. was born in South Philadelphia. He was the son of a legendary Common Pleas Court Judge, G. Fred DiBona, and the former Rose D'Amico—the woman described by her son as "the soul of our family."

Following graduation from South Philadelphia High School and Davis and Elkins College, He earned a law degree from the Delaware School of Law. His career in the business was a combination of public and private service. From untangling the bureaucracy of the city's zoning board, to invigorating the local Chamber of Commerce, to transforming a health insurance plan into one of the nation's leading managed care companies he demonstrated his significant leadership.

At just 25 years old, he assumed the chairmanship of the Philadelphia Zoning Board of Adjustment, an agency all but paralyzed by a six-month backlog of cases. By the time Mr. DiBona relinquished the job three years later, cases were moving through the board in just 18 days. His then moved to the Philadelphia Port Corporation, where for three years he served as President. His tenure saw the corporation transform itself from a landlord for riverfront property into a full-service marketing operation.

In 1983, Mr. DiBona assumed the presidency of the Greater Philadelphia Chamber of Commerce and led the business association through the greatest period of growth in its history. In just three years, the Chamber increased its membership from 1,800 businesses to 4,800. In addition, Mr. DiBona was credited with dramatically increasing the organization's political clout, leading the Chamber's successful lobbying efforts in Harrisburg to support funding for a new Convention Center in Philadelphia.

In 1986, Mr. DiBona ended speculation that he might be a candidate for mayor by moving into the private sector, where he entered the revolution that was overtaking America's health care system. He led Independence Blue Cross as President and CEO for fifteen years and the company through a very difficult transformation. The company realized significant growth in both revenue and profits and he was widely recognized as a very successful CEO.

As the success of Independence Blue Cross grew, so did the national profile of its chief executive. During the mid-1990s, Mr. DiBona served consecutive terms as Chairman of the Blue Cross and Blue Shield Association, the country's largest association of private health insurers. He also is a former member of the Harvard Health Policy and Management Executive Council, a think tank group at the Harvard School of Public Health. His business and management expertise was often sought out by CEOs and leaders of companies and not-for-profit organizations. They ranged from neighborhood-based organizations to Fortune 500 companies.

Mr. DiBona was on the boards of Aqua America Inc. (formerly Philadelphia Suburban Corporation); Crown Holdings, Inc., Exelon Corporation, The GEO Group, Inc. and Tasty Baking Company. In addition, he served on the boards of a number of not-for-profit organizations including the Peter Nero and Philly Pops Board, which he chaired.

But for Mr DiBona, business fortunes only provided one measure of his company's success; equally important was IBC's dedication to a Social Mission—a commitment to investing IBC's people and resources in the overall health of the Philadelphia region. For Mr. DiBona, Social Mission took on a variety of forms, such as providing 150,000 needy children with health insurance over 15 years through the Caring Foundation, which he founded during his first year at IBC; to granting $6 million in financial assistance to the region's Charitable Medical Clinics; to encouraging the volunteer efforts of hundreds of IBC "Blue Crew" members in all manner of worthy causes.

Mr. DiBona also invited experts to his office one day to address the nursing shortage problem and asked, "How can IBC best help?" Their answer, he said, surprised him: "We need more nursing teachers. We're turning away nursing students because we need teachers." In response, IBC launched its Nurse Scholars Program, a three-year commitment of $3 million for nursing scholarships. In its first year alone, the program—administered in partnership with the Pennsylvania Higher Education Foundation—provided financial aid to nearly 600 graduate and undergraduate students in nursing or nursing education.

His community honors included: in 1995, along with former President George Bush, the National Patriot's Award from the Congressional Medal of Honor Society; in 1996, the Thomas Cahill Leadership Award for his efforts in economic development from Roman Catholic High School, and the Jewish National Fund Tree of Life Award; in 1997, the Annual Business Leadership Award from LaSalle University; in 1998, the "Good Scout" award of the Cradle of Liberty Council, Boy Scouts of America; and in 2002, the 95th Annual Whitney M. Young, Jr. Leadership Award from the Urban League of Philadelphia.

Sadly, Fred DiBona died on January 11, 2005 after a courageous fight with cancer while this book was being written. He was 53. He will be missed by all.

John DiIulio Jr.

John DiIulio Jr. had been announced in February of 2001 by President George Bush to head the United States Office of Faith-Based and Community Initiatives. His mission was to weed out federal laws that unnecessarily block community and faith-based social welfare organizations from competing for federal dollars. His job was also to test, with statistic precision and academic vigor, the power of the "Faith factor" to solve social problems.

John was born on Morris Street in South Philadelphia in a narrow three-story row house in the St Thomas Aquinas Parish. When John finished the second grade, his parents moved to a row house in southwest Philadelphia's Saint Barnabas Parish. He won a scholarship to the Haverford School in Delaware County and from there he went to the University of Pennsylvania. He received his PhD from Harvard in 1986 and immediately received a job offer from Princeton. The school offered him tenure after only two years. Five years after he received his doctorate, Princeton offered him a full professor position. He was only thirty-two years old.

His credentials include being an advisor to Vice President Gore on reinventing government. During the 2000 campaign, he consulted with both the Bush and the Gore teams before each candidate gave major speeches on faith-based initiatives.

For this graduate of St Barnabas parish school, subsidiary means "it's better to get help from your family, your friends and your neighbors. If you cannot get it from them, it's really good to get it from the church or some other local groups. And if you cannot fix it there, your city government should be ready to stand by you. And if that is not enough, Harrisburg or Lansing, will be there. And, ultimately, there's no shame, there is nothing wrong, you should not be worried about going to Washington, D.C. and the Federal government for help."

He is a controversial person with very distinctive views about these subjects. But nonetheless a person values and deep roots in his Italian-American heritage and desire to improve the community we share.

Susan Molinari

Susan Molinari has also devoted a good portion of her life to serving others. Susan is the Chairman of the Century Council, a not-for profit organization dedicated to fighting drunk driving and under age drinking, and funded by America's leading distillers. In addition she chairs the Ripon Educational Fund and is the spokesperson for the Americans for Consumer Education and Competition, which is a financial literacy organization. She also served on the Bush-Cheney Transition Advisory Committee.

She also served on several boards including Protective Life Insurance, The Toyota North America Diversity Advisory Board, the March of Dimes Advisory Board, and the National Italian American Foundation.

Susan was born and raised on Staten Island. Her grandfather was an Italian-American immigrant elected to the New York State Assembly and she was elected to Congress succeeding her father, Guy V. Molinari. She was a member of Congress from 1990 to 1997. In 1994, after only four years in Congress, she was elected by her peers to the eight-person Republican Majority Leadership, making her the highest-ranking women in Congress at the time.

In 1997, she left Congress to co-anchor CBS News Saturday Morning Show, where she conducted on-air interviews with national and international newsmakers.

Leon Panetta

Leo Panetta has a long and distinguished career in government ranging from his time in the United States Army to his service as Chief of Staff to the President of the United States. Panetta was born in Monterey, California on June 28, 1938 of Italian immigrant parents. He attended both Catholic and public schools while he worked on his family farm in Carmel Valley. He received his undergraduate degree from Santa Clara University in 1960 and his Juris Doctorate from Santa Clara University Law School in 1963, where he was the editor of the Law Review.

His first position in Washington in 1966 was as a legislative assistant to U.S. Senator Thomas H. Kuchel of California, the Senate Minority Whip. In 1969, he became the Special Assistant to the Secretary to the Secretary of Health, Education and Welfare and then Director of the U. S. Office for Civil Rights.

Panetta was the U.S. Representative from California's 16th (now 17th) district from 1977 to 1993. He left Congress in 1993 to become Director of the Office of Management and Budget for the incoming Clinton administration. He was appointed President Clinton's Chief of Staff on July 17, 1994 and served in that position until January 20, 1997.

While he has left politics, he continues his life of service. Along with his wife Sylvia, Panetta co-directs the Leo and Sylvia Panetta Institute for Public Policy, based at California State University, Monterey Bay—a University that he helped to establish on the site of a former military base. The institute serves as a non-profit study center for the advancement of public policy to help our communities and our country meet the challenges of the next century.

Panetta's awards and honors include the NEA Lincoln Award, the A. Philip Randolph Award, the President's Award, and the Peter Burnett Award for Distinguished Public Service, The Distinguished Public Service Medal, and the Special Achievement Award for Public Service from the National Italian American Foundation.

Brian Piccolo

Other people serve others even when it is to their own determent. An example of this is the now famous story of Brian Piccolo. Louis Brian Piccolo was born in Pittsfield, Mass. However, he spent most of his years growing up in Fort Lauderdale, Florida. He attended Wake Forest University. In 1964, his senior year, he led the nation in rushing.

Despite the fact that he was the leading rusher that year, he was not picked in the National Football league draft. Two hundred and eighty picks and no team chose him. They thought he was too small and too slow for the NFL. However, after the draft, Bears owner George Halas stepped in and signed Piccolo as a free agent. He spent 1965 on the Bears practice squad. In 1966, he rushed 3 times for 12 yards. In 1967, he rushed for 317 yards and caught passes for 103 yards. In 1968 he got his opportunity, Gayle Sayers, the Bears star, suffered a massive knee injury at the hands of 49er Kermit Alexander. He was lost for the season, and the "Pic" stepped in. In the last five games, Brian gained 450 yards on the ground and 281 in the air. He also scored his first two NFL touchdowns.

During the 1968 off-season, Sayers became the first player to successfully return to football from such a massive knee injury. Piccolo assisted Sayers both mentally and physically throughout the rehabilitation. Despite the fact that Piccolo would lose his starting role, he was Sayers biggest supporter for his return to health. With Sayers returning, Brian again was second string and he had other problems.

On November 16, 1969, in Atlanta, Brian took himself out of the game because he could not breathe. After several days of tests, Brian was diagnosed with embryonal cell carcinoma as mediastinal teratoma (a type of cancer found as a large tumor in his chest cavity).

As many readers know by reading the popular book, *Brian Piccolo, A Short Season*, and the seeing the movie *Brian's Song*, it was only a matter of time before

Brian died heroically on June 16, 1970 at he age of 26 leaving his wife and three daughters.

Dominic Renzulli

Not all people who providing service to others are famous. There are millions of people out there every day doing great things that may not get the attention but they are doing wonders. Dominic Renzulli is an example.

He is not famous but an estimated 500 people gathered at St Francis of Assisi Church in Weston, CT. on June 15, 2000 as the Weston Volunteer Fire Department gave a "fireman's funeral" to Dominic Renzulli, the "best guy ever."

Dominic was born in Norwalk, CT. on May 27, 1928. He was the son of Americo and Caroline Romei Renzulli. He was one of the owners of the Renzulli Brothers Garden Center and in 1965; he and his brothers became partners in a real estate business, Renzulli Associates Properties. However, throughout his life, he was a man of service to his community. He was a life member to the Weston, CT. Volunteer Fire Department where he served for thirty-three years. He was a member of the Weston Emergency Medical Service and a founding member of the Weston Boosters Club. He was named Weston Citizen of the Year in 1986. He was not famous but he was loved by all those that he helped throughout the years.

Jimmy Martello

Jimmy Martello wrote a lot of checks he did not have to write to people that he believed need his help. He wrote checks to friends that were in need of extra cash and a stranger who had a brain tumor and three children who were in need of the necessities of life. Jimmy took on whatever he could around the neighborhood: installing cabinets, fixing broken windows, landscaping the front yard. He coached football and roller hockey.

He was an ordinary middle class guy from New Jersey. That is if you can call someone "ordinary" who was 6'3" and weighs 240 pounds and was a varsity linebacker at Rutgers University and an impressively successful trader at Cantor Fitzgerald. It is reported in the newspapers that he played middle linebacker for the Scarlet Knights. Though his team during his senior year struggled through a

5-6 season, family members recalled Mr. Martello played his best game in a 47-3 loss against the University of Pittsburgh and their All-American quarterback, Dan Marino. It was also reported in that same newspaper that his credo, said his wife, Sheila, was, "If it needs to be loved, love it; if it needs to be given, give it; if it needs to be done, do it."

Jimmy, who was born in Brooklyn, was planning to teach his boys—James Jr., 7, and Thomas, 5—to fish and water ski. The family would go boating next summer he planned Those dreams vanished Sept. 11 when a hijacked plane dove into One World Trade Center, where Jimmy worked as a partner and equity sales trader for Cantor Fitzgerald Securities. He worked on the 104th floor.

SERVICE ORGANIZATIONS

UNICO

UNICO is a National Italian Service Organization and one of the early Italian service organizations. Its Brookhaven Chapter, founded on December 29, 1969, is one example of the success of this national organization. This Chapter's membership works very hard each year to pool their resources and contribute to the variety of causes and charities within their community.

They award a number of scholarships in the names of such noted Italian-Americans like Sergeant John Basilone, William Davini, Major Don Gentile, Alphonse Miele, Theodore Mazza, and Dr. Benjamin Cottone. The local chapter supports charities such as Cooley's Anemia, Good Shepard Hospice, Hope House, The Italian American Immigrant Museums of Italy and the Make a Wish Foundation.

Augustus Society

Augustus Society is an organization of Italian-American Professionals and Executives that offers scholarships, awareness, and assistance programs to those in need in their community of Clark County, Nevada. The organization was founded in 1983 and since it was founded it has awarded approximately 382 scholarships to needy students totally over $600,000.

They hold an Annual Scholarship Banquet honoring the students and their parents each April and they also sponsor a Columbus Day Ball where they also honor an *Italian American Person of the Year.*

The Massachusetts Italian American Police Officer Association

The Massachusetts Italian American Police Officer Association was founded in 1968 when three Boston Police Officers formed a group to provide fellowship and common support for members of law enforcement of Italian heritage. Since that beginning The Massachusetts Association of Italian American Police Officers has distinguished itself as one of the finest ethnic organizations in the New England area and one of the largest ethnic law enforcement organizations in the state.

The association annually awards scholarships to the children of members of the association. Each year they award scholarships to sons and daughters of their members who are attending a qualified college or university. In 2004, ten students received these scholarships from this Association. They support many charitable events including Neighbors In Need, Homeless Veterans, Jimmy Fund, Law Enforcement Memorial, Honoring our officer's who paid the supreme sacrifice.

Italian American Police Society of New Jersey

Italian American Police Society of New Jersey is fraternal organization of more then 4,500 Italian-American Law Enforcement Officers in the State of New Jersey. In addition to their fraternal goal, their mission is to promote their Italian heritage through helping the community as well as helping all the law enforcement members and their families.

Each spring they hold an Annual Scholarship Breakfast where they present ten $1,000 memorial scholarships in memory of the Italian-American Police Officers that lost their lives in the line of duty. They also present awards to members for valor, meritorious service, and heroism. During Christmas, the society hosts a party for the Big Brothers & Big Sisters of New Jersey where they distribute toys to all the needy children. They also work in homeless shelters to distribute more then six truckloads of toys.

NYPD Columbia Association

NYPD Columbia Association is a not-for-profit fraternal association of Italian-American police officers of the New York City Police Department. Like a number of Italian-American organizations today, this organization is also growing its' membership and expects to do so again in 2005. While it is primarily a fraternal organization, it also provides high school and college scholarships to it's' members and donations to various charities and educational institutions in their communities.

At one event, for example, proceeds went to St. Patrick's Nursing Home, Calvary Hospital, Providence Rest Nursing Home, Pace University, and Loyola College.

Italian American Brotherhood Club

In the 1920's, the Italian American Brotherhood Club was originally established as a social club. Currently, the Italian American Brotherhood Club (IABC) is a social service agency undergoing a Rinascimento, a Rebirth! The IABC has been reorganized exclusively for charitable, religious, educational and scientific purposes. Active in the Italian American Community, the IABC is officially a 501-C3 exempt organization. During this exciting era, the IABC has awarded more than $100,000 in scholarships to deserving students. The IABC has also supported Holy Rosary Montessori School, the D.A.R.E Program and the Alta House.

The IABC has honored several of northeast Ohio's Italian-American's by hosting annual "Honoree of the Year" dinners. Past recipients have included Bishop Anthony Pilla, Vince Marotta, Bedford Heights Mayor Jimmy Dimora, Common Pleas Judge Anthony O' Calabrese, Judge Joseph Zingales, Vince Campanella, Paul Russo, Sam Rutigliano, Nick Orlando Sr and Cuyahoga County Common Pleas Judge Frank D. Celebrezze, Jr. Cuyahoga County Auditor Frank Russo and Martin Vittardi.

In it's seventy fourth year, the goal of the Italian American Brotherhood Club remains dedicated to support, plan, develop, provide, and operate a social service organization which will serve a public purpose and provide for the needy as well as afford educational opportunities through a continuing scholarship program.

These individuals and organizations truly represent the true Italian-American value of providing service to others in our community who are in need of our assistance. Our history has many examples of this and our future will bring many more.

13

The Value of Entrepreneurship

One of the greatest talents demonstrated by many Italian-Americans in the United States has been their ability to provide a living for themselves and their families. Ever since the great migration they have a history of setting up independent businesses and proven to be able to earn a living for themselves and others. Growing up in my neighborhood, I saw family businesses all around me. Many businesses such as people cleaning clothing, sewing, selling dresses, insurance and other things were transacted right out of the family home.

My father would actually tell me stories about the days when families would run restaurants in their homes. I don't remember any restaurants in people's homes but I do remember people selling clothing, doing tailoring, repairing shoes, selling produce, and catering out of their houses. It was a very entrepreneurial environment. I am sure there are many governmental regulations against a number of those practices now.

But my most exciting memories are about the businesses on Ninth Street in South Philadelphia. That place was electrifying. While the businesses on Ninth Street were local that catered to the local residents, not all businesses that were founded by Italian-Americans stayed small but many did start that way.

We will talk about Ninth Street in another section of this book but just let me say that Donald Trump could have learned a lot as an apprentice there when he was a teenager.

In this section, we will talk about some Italian-Americans who used hard work, determination, and very little money created some very successful companies. We will only discuss just a few companies and their founders as examples. There are plenty more. The point is that the values instilled in these founders by their Italian-American immigrant parents helped them create these companies. The companies then created jobs for many Americans and significant financial value for the United States economy. The first company is Tropicana.

<u>Tropicana</u>

Italian immigrant Anthony Rossi founded the company that became Tropicana in 1947 when he realized that the town of Bradenton, Florida was an ideal location for a citrus business. Rossi had a dream of sharing the Florida's citrus fruit with the people living outside the state. In doing so, he changed the way Northerners bought and enjoyed Florida citrus forever.

In the late 1940s, Anthony Rossi was an entrepreneur in search of the ideal business. He was always interested in fine food, presented to please the eye as well as the palate. So, with typical Rossi artistry and care he began to prepare gift boxes of Florida citrus. Soon he was selling the boxes to department stores, including Macy's and Gimbel's in New York City. At his first manufacturing plant, Anthony employed fifty people, mostly women. They cut the fresh fruit by hand over stainless steel counters and packed it carefully into glass jars.

First they placed layers of grapefruit sections in the jars and then oranges over the grapefruit. In the "fruit salad" jars, they added slices of pineapple. The attention to detail became the hallmark of the company. Shipping fresh fruit segments and juice to the Northeast proved so successful that Mr. Rossi discontinued production of his fruit gift boxes. But another revolution was dawning for the citrus industry.

The post-World War II era was ushering in the baby boom and the growth of the suburbs. Busy families kept their new refrigerator-freezers stocked with frozen dinners and, beginning in the late 1940s, frozen concentrated orange juice.

In the fast-growing processed food industry of the 1950s, this new company from Bradenton, Florida was introducing new innovative ways of doing things in the industry. For example, frozen concentrated juice packages, emblazoned with the lively character of Tropic-Ana, were consumer favorites in supermarket cases across America. To comply with its goal of using every part of the fruit, the company invested in machinery to convert citrus peel, pulp and seeds into nutritional cattle feed.

Throughout his career, Mr. Rossi led Tropicana to be an innovator in the industry. It was the first to introduce frozen concentrated orange juice packages, emblazoned with the lively character of Tropic-Ana that were consumer favorites in supermarket cases across America.

In the 1950s, they commissioned American Can Company to develop a waxed paper carton in half pint, pint and quart sizes. One million dollars' worth of refrigerated trucks bought. The risk was high on a new product with no real understanding of the magnitude of consumer acceptance there would be from the public from this new product. Soon the juice was being distributed across the country. Every morning, two thousand dairies were delivering cartons of Tropicana orange juice to the doorsteps of their customers.

The company also introduced the world's only orange juice tank ship, the SS Tropicana. At peak capacity, the ship carried 1.5 million gallons of orange juice from Florida to New York each week-helping launch Tropicana's leadership in the American food industry.

In 1961 the SS Tropicana made its final voyage delivering chilled orange juice to New York. While the ship could get Tropicana's products to market quickly, the juice still had to be put into cartons in New York. So the company found a way to package its juice at Tropicana headquarters, and then ship the packaged product directly from Bradenton.

Tropicana Products, Inc. was first sold over the counter in 1969. The company was soon listed on the New York Stock Exchange. In 1978 Beatrice acquired Tropicana Products, Inc.

Brutocao Engineering & Construction, Inc.

Brothers Albert and Leonard Brutocao started Brutocao Engineering & Construction, Inc. in Concord California on January 27th 1967. Their first job was a slide repair project on the University of California Berkley campus. On June 8th, 1968 the decision was made to move to Covina and start their business in Southern California. Their next project was in the Inland Empire constructing a bridge and channel for the County of San Bernardino in Chino. During the 1970's Brutocao built bridges in Fullerton, Carson, Los Angeles, Long Beach, Van Nuys,

Bakersfield, North Hollywood, Santa Monica, Cucamonga, Thousand Oaks, and Huntington Beach. To date, Brutocao has completed work on over 350 projects with a combined value of over a billion dollars.

Brutocao had been working out of a job trailer in Covina California until they need more space and in 1981, the company moved to their present location in Fontana California. The Fontana office sits on a seven-acre site and serves as the headquarters for Brutocao as well as the equipment and maintenance yard.

Brutocao Engineering has maintained a strong sense of commitment to its employees; the industry; and the community. The company, when started, was based on these values as well as their strong family values and they continue to follow them to this day. Len Brutocao, CEO, told me two stories that demonstrate how they stayed true to these values at all costs.

Early in their history, the company had four proposals with one major potential customer. They needed the work very badly and hoped to get at least two of the projects. Len met with the potential buyer and he told Len that Len would get the work if he would give the buyer a "kick back". Len was told that his competitor was willing to do so. Len refused and lost all of the four projects but he kept his integrity.

On another occasion, Len was asked by a buyer for a new set of golf clubs in exchange for his approval to do the work. Len did buy the golf clubs but instead of giving them to the buyer, Len brought the clubs to the President of the company, i.e. the buyer's boss. Len showed the President the clubs and told him what the buyer had said. The buyer was fired.

These are stories of integrity. Len and Albert built their company on the Italian-American values that were taught by their parents and Len still manages his companies that way today.

Planters Peanuts

Amedeo Obici was the founder of Planters Peanuts. He was born in 1876 in the small town of Oderzo near Venice, Italy. His father died when he was a child.

When Obici was old enough to read, his widowed mother would show him his uncle's glowing letters from America. Thus began Obici's dream. At age eleven, reality had him pulling up at Bush Terminal in Brooklyn, New York. He arrived in America at 11 years old, not knowing any English, but going on to become a prosperous business innovator.

His willingness to work showed even at this early age. He started his career as a bellhop and fruit stand vendor in Scranton, Pennsylvania. Later, Obici moved to Wilkes-Barre, Pennsylvania and opened his own fruit stand and invested in a peanut roaster. Here he linked his life's fortune with the peanut. In a few years, Obici turned peddler, using a horse and wagon, and called himself: The Peanut Specialist.

In 1906, Obici went into partnership with Mario Peruzzi, He had developed his own method of blanching whole roasted peanuts, doing away with the troublesome hulls and skins; and so with six employees two large roasters, and crude machinery, Planters was founded. Amedeo Obici realized that prices and first profits were not nearly so important as repeat business and proved his operation based on quality and brand name were important for continued success. Two years later, the firm was incorporated as Planters Nut and Chocolate Company.

In 1916, at forty, Obici and Louise Musante were married. She also had been an operator of a small peanut stand in Wilkes-Barre, Pennsylvania. Business growth accelerated, so Obici opened a Planters factory in Suffolk, Virginia. The married couple began to think of Suffolk as home and listed their legal residence as Bay Point Dairy Farm, a 260-acre estate on the Nansemond River about 10 miles from Suffolk.

Years earlier, he had saved enough money to help his family emigrate from Italy to the U.S. Obici was a generous benefactor, especially to the town of Suffolk. He endowed a hospital for the town to memorialize his beloved Louise. Even today, the hospital is helped by this one man who had come so far—Amedeo Obici, the founder of Planters.

Obici Hospital, 138-bed state-of-the-art facility, is located on Godwin Boulevard in Suffolk. Opened in April 2002, the new facility continues a 50-year tradition of providing residents of Suffolk and Western Tidewater with patient-centered care in an environment that focuses on healing.

Prince Spaghetti Company

In 1912, Three Sicilian immigrants: Gaetano LaMarco, Guiseppe Seminara and Michele Cantella, decided to open a small spaghetti manufacturing company on Prince Street in Boston. They never dreamed their business would become one of the largest pasta companies in the nation. However, together, the three men felt they had the skills needed to be successful so they were very comfortable in their roles. Mr. LaMarca was the administrator; Mr. Seminara was the salesman; and Mr. Cantella was the manufacturer.

In the early years, they manufactured macaroni on the second floor of 92 Prince Street. They later extended to the next building. By 1917 they expanded and built a 7-story structure. Construction included a railroad track that entered into the back of the building along Atlantic Avenue. The semolina used in the macaroni was transported on these railroad cars and was unloaded directly inside. Twenty years later, they had outgrown that building and again needed more space. Mr. LaMarca spent several years surveying many sites, and then with the cooperation of all the partners, made the move to Lowell.

Prince moved to Lowell in 1939. Guiseppe Pellegrino, another Sicilian immigrant, became involved with Prince in 1940. At that time the three original founders needed additional assistance. In 1940, with a seemingly limitless capacity for work and a knack for publicity The young man had come to Lowell looking for a pasta mill to replace the mill that his wife's family had lost in a Brooklyn, N.Y. fire.

The new plant impressed young Pellegrino so much that he actually moved into a room there until he could raise enough money to buy control of the company a year later. The cost was a few thousand dollars. Advertising for the company during the period before the 1950s was mainly done in Italian newspapers since spaghetti and macaroni were considered an ethnic food. Around 1953, Mr. Pellegrino hired the advertising firm of Jerome O'Leary of Boston where they created the famous slogan "Wednesday is Prince Spaghetti Day." This was an attempt to introduce non-Italians to pasta products. The advertising at this time was done on radio.

Prince sponsored "The Stan Freberg Show"; and later did television commercials sponsoring the Sunday Night Movie of the Week. This was a big advancement for Prince. Joseph P. Pellegrino II continued to take an active part in the business in the early 1960s with aggressive advertising and promotions. In 1969, the famous "Anthony" TV commercial was introduced to the public.

One fall afternoon in 1969, 12-year-old Anthony Martignetti was standing on a street corner near his family's North End home when he was approached by two men who were filming a commercial for Prince Spaghetti. The camera followed Anthony as he ran through narrow alleyways. By the end of the day, the commercial was born. There are few who watched television in New England in the 1970s who do not remember the familiar refrain of a woman peering out a tenement window, yelling for Anthony to come home for a supper of Prince Spaghetti

Joseph P. Pellegrino II took over from his father and became Prince's President in 1973. The company was sold to Borden in 1987 for $164 million.

Luigino's, Inc.

Jeno F. Paulucci, Founder and Chairman of Luigino's, Inc., and creator of its Michelina's brand is frequently called "The Incomparable Entrepreneur." When he was 85 he still worked seven days a week. He has created more than 70 brands; built and sold companies worth more than $2 billion in today's dollars—companies such as the Chun King Corporation, Northland Foods, Inc.; the worldwide Cornelius Company, Jeno's, Inc., City of Heathrow, and others. Jeno Francesco Paulucci is the son of Italian immigrants. His father, Ettore, found work in the iron mines and his mother, Michelina, operated a small grocery in their home in Hibbing, Minnesota.

Born as a child of the Great Depression, Jeno helped his dirt-poor family survive by selling fruits and vegetables in a local market at age 10. Thus he began a lifetime foods industry career which led him to create, finance or lead more than 50 privately held companies and organizations in a career spanning 70 years of entrepreneurship, which continues to this day.

His energy created the Chun King Divider Pak and Jeno's Pizza Rolls, which revolutionized the foods industry. He pioneered domestication of wild rice on his 5,000 acres of Wilderness Farms in Northeastern Minnesota; launched RJR Foods Inc. (later RJR-Nabisco) as it's founding Chairman, and is the creative mind behind dozens of patents for processes to prepare and package foods. His Luigino's, Inc., producers of Michelina's (named for his mother) and Budget Gourmet brands, is one of the world's leading packers of frozen entrees. Based on his credo that "jobs are the funnel from which flow the benefits of a better over-all economy for all," in 1990 he arranged financing from city, county, state and federal sources so that he had zero investment in this start-up company.

Jeno wanted to prove that an entrepreneur with a good track record, whose word was his bond, could trade jobs as a commodity for low-interest loans, but never outright dollar grants, from local and federal government agencies. As a result, since 1990 Jeno has created and now operates five foods companies producing frozen entrees, hand-held snacks, pizza, and food service products for worldwide markets with cash flow over $100 million a year.

Hanna-Barbera Studio

The partnership between Bill Hanna and Joe Barbera goes back much farther than Hanna-Barbera Studio. It began in 1939, when they teamed up to co-direct cartoons for MGM. Their first release, *Puss Gets the Boot* (1940), introduced their first pair of famous characters—a cat named Jasper and an unnamed mouse, who quickly became Tom & Jerry. It also gave the pair their first Oscar nomination.

Their tenure at MGM lasted until 1957, the year MGM decided to get out of the cartoon business and Hanna and Barbera went out on their own and directed over 100 Tom & Jerry shorts, seven of which won Academy Awards. The fledgling studio had cartoons on the air within months. *Ruff & Reddy* was a series of shorts much like they'd always done, except less expensively produced. It was packaged for TV just like the old theatrical cartoons, too, one of three segments in a half-hour show.

This gave the producers less control over their own work than they could have if they were handling the entire show—a factor they quickly moved to eliminate. From their second production, *Huckleberry Hound* on, the studio has produced nothing but complete shows. To cut production costs to the bone, Hanna and Barbera worked out a system of what they called "planned animation". Instead of animating an entire figure, only those body parts that moved were animated, with the rest held steady—that way, most of the body could be treated as background, with one drawing sufficing for an entire scene.

They made a breakthrough in 1960 with *The Flintstones,* the first successful prime time animated series ever to be broadcast by an American TV network. It sparked a brief fad in prime-time animation. In 1964, Hanna-Barbera released its first feature, *Hey There, It's Yogi Bear.* The studio has released dozens of features since; including *The Man Called Flintstone, Yogi's First Christmas* and *The Jetsons Meet the Flintstones.* In 1991 the studio was acquired by cable mogul Ted Turner.

Blimpie International, Inc

Anthony Conza, Founder, Chairman and CEO of Blimpie International, Inc. founded the Blimpie restaurant chain in 1964, with two friends in Hoboken, New Jersey, with no money, a simple idea and a lot of passion. Today, Blimpie International has approximately 2000 franchises with system-wide sales approaching $400 million in all 50 states and 12 foreign countries.

Mr. Conza is known to millions through the Blimpie television and radio commercials. He has also been a guest on several television business and news programs and has been in The Wall Street Journal and other business periodicals. Mr. Conza is a member of the Board of Governors of the Boys & Girls Clubs of America where, as chairman of their marketing committee, he has been responsible for creating the popular public service announcements featuring Colin Powell and Denzel Washington. He also serves on the Dean's Council at Harvard University's Kennedy School of Government.

He is the recipient of the Ernst & Young/Inc. Magazine "Entrepreneur of the Year" Award, the New York State Restaurant Association's "Chain of the Year" Award, the Boys & Girls Clubs of America's "President's Award" and the Ellis Island "Medal of Honor."

Diamond Comic Distributors, Inc.

Stephen A. Geppi, is the President and CEO, of Diamond Comic Distributors, Inc. Diamond is an international comic book, toy and book distribution business. He was born in the "Little Italy" section of Baltimore, has risen high in business but his friends will tell you that he has never lost sight of the importance of faith, family and community service.

Mr. Geppi entered the comics business in 1974 when he opened Geppi's Comic World. He soon expanded to four stores. By 1982, his distributor was failing and he decided to move into distribution as well. In just over a decade's time Mr. Geppi expanded his comic book distribution business across North America and Europe. After more than 20 years, Diamond is the world's largest distributor of English-language comics and related merchandise, with a network of distribution centers throughout the world.

Today Diamond Comic Distributors serves as the exclusive distributor for many of the comic industry's leading publishers including DC Comics, Marvel Comics, Dark Horse Comics and Image Comics. Diamond has also expanded into the toy and book distribution businesses with the successful start-up of Diamond Select Toys and Diamond Book Distributors.

In addition to his distribution businesses, Mr. Geppi moved into the publishing arena with the creation of Gemstone Publishing, Inc. and now publishes The Overstreet Comic Book Price Guide, "the comic industry's bible of pricing" for back issues. Today, Gemstone also publishes classic character Disney Comics. In January of 1995, he opened Diamond International Galleries, which is has an array of comics, original comic art, posters, animation cells and backgrounds, drawings, oils, antique toys—a comprehensive inventory of collectibles and memorabilia.

Sally Beauty Supply

Sally Beauty Supply has been guided by Michael H. Renzulli, president and chief executive officer since 1972. A trained pharmacist, he spent his youth and the beginning of his career in his father's Philadelphia drugstore. Sally Beauty Supply began as one store in New Orleans in 1964. Under his direction, through a series of acquisitions and new store openings in the 1970s, 80s and 90s and ongoing, the company now owns and operates more than 2,750 worldwide.

Today, Sally Beauty Company is the world's largest distributor of professional beauty supplies. Sally currently owns and operates Sally Beauty Supply stores 48 states, Puerto Rico, Japan, Germany, the United Kingdom, Mexico and Canada.

Subway

Fred DeLuca was a seventeen year old boy in "the projects" in Bridgeport, Connecticut. It was the summer of 1965 and Fred had just graduated from high school and his thoughts were about going to college but he had no money. During the summer of '65, there wasn't that much hopes that the eldest DeLuca child would have enough money to pay for his college tuition. He was a hard working, competent and dependable; but the $1.25-per-hour minimum wage job that he had at the local hardware store could not pay for a college education.

In July, 1965, during a barbecue at the home of a family friend Dr. Peter Buck, that a business relationship was forged between young Fred DeLuca and Dr. Buck that would forever change the landscape of the fast food industry. At the barbecue, Fred thought about asking Dr. Buck for a loan for college but Dr. Buck offered Fred a business proposition instead. Dr, Buck suggested that he open a submarine shop. He offered him $1,000 investment to be his partner.

Their goal was to open 32 submarine sandwich shops within 10 years. By 1974 they owned and operated 16 units throughout the state of Connecticut. It seemed unlikely that they would double that number in two years. DeLuca has concentrated on expanding Subway Restaurants.

On a Monday night in 1974, Buck and DeLuca met with their attorney. They discussed the future of their business. They evaluated their options, talk turned to franchising. Franchising, they had previously thought, was for the big companies and had dismissed the idea. Now, being behind schedule, they were willing to look into it. All there was to do was recruit people who would invest their money and use Pete and Fred's management system to open and run Subway restaurants in their hometown. DeLuca figured that the fastest way to expand the business was to go out and find a franchisee so he spoke to his friend Brian Dixon. He told him about their franchising plans and offered to loan him the money to buy their restaurant located in Wallingford, Conn.

Dixon refused. He was used to getting a paycheck every week and didn't want to risk going into business. DeLuca devoted his time to managing their existing restaurants and decided to worry later about franchising. One day, Brian Dixon changed his mind. When he reported to work that morning, he was shocked to discover a padlock on his boss's office and a sheriff's note that stated that the business was closed. It was bankrupt. Brian didn't panic. Somewhere in that sheriff's notice, he saw the word "opportunity" and decided to call DeLuca and take him up on his previous offer to become the very first Subway franchisee. From that day forward, not only did Dixon's life change, so did the way that Subway did business.

In the year 2004, the Subway chain is in its 39th year of operation. It is the world's largest submarine sandwich chain with more than 21,000 restaurants in 75 countries.

These are just a few examples of the companies founded by enterprising Italian-Americans. They do make my point. These are people who had a dream and with some hard work and the desire to succeed made it happen even with little money despite the odds.

14

The Value Service to Your Country

Another strong value taught within the Italian-American family was dedication and service to your country. The Italian immigrants came from a very different kind of government and they truly appreciated the differences here in the United States. My grandfather would talk for hours about the oppression of the individual in Europe compared to here in the United States, for example.

Throughout my life, my grandparents recounted the differences between the United States and Europe and told me how they cherished the freedoms and values that this country stood for. They emphasized the importance of fighting to keep those freedoms at any cost. There was no question, from any early age on, that my brother and I were going to enlist in the Armed Services when we were of age. We were going to "do our time in the serve of our country". And we did.

My father had served in World War II. My Grandfather had served in World War I. In our community, it was an obligation for every boy to serve some time in the armed services when they reached the appropriate age. The Italian-American neighborhoods had their share of war heroes also. Take John Basilone and Dominic Gentile for examples.

<u>Sergeant John Basilone</u>

Sergeant Basilone received the Congressional Medal of Honor for his gallant action during the Battle of Guadalcanal in 1942 and the Navy Cross posthumously for heroism in the Battle of Iwo Jima where he was killed in 1945. John was born on November 4, 1916. He grew up in Raritan, New Jersey. John never attended high school; he was too adventurous to sit still for that. After a few years trying to find himself, he joined the Army in 1934 and did a tour of duty in the Philippines. After his tour ended in 1937, John returned home to Raritan.

But John became restless again and longed for the life of a soldier. This time he joined the Marines. In August 1942, 10 months into World War II for the U.S., his group was sent to Guadalcanal. The United States and Japanese were fighting for possession of the island. The marines were greatly outnumbered. John Basilone was in charge of 16 men. They set up a defensive position with the 4 machine guns in front of Henderson Field which was the airfield that they were instructed to defend. Throughout heavy attacks by the enemy John led his men and he risked his life to get much need ammunition through heavy arms fire.

That night, October 24th & the morning of October 25th, the United States had turned the tide of the war in the Pacific and the previously undefeated Japanese were on their way to defeat thanks to John and the other Marines on that island. For his heroics, John was awarded The Congressional Medal of Honor. John died on February 19, 1945, while leading an effort to stop Japanese soldiers from shooting at Marines from a bunker on Iwo Jima. On that day, John gathered some troops and weapons and started across the beach. He was hit by a Japanese mortar shell. He died within thirty minutes. For his actions that day, John was awarded The Navy Cross.

<u>Major Don Gentile</u>

Major Don Gentile shot down over thirty Nazi planes during World War II. Eisenhower called him a "one man Air Force" and personally pinned the Distinguished Service Cross on him. He was born in Piqua, Ohio on December 6, 1920. Even as a child, he had this fascination for airplanes and this dream to fly. He logged three hundred hours flight time by July 1941.

Don was thinking about joining the United States Air Force. However, that required that he attend two years of college to qualify for flight training before he could be admitted. He joined the Royal Canadian Air Force instead where no such requirement existed. In September 1942, Don Gentile transferred into the United States Army and was assigned to the 336th Fighter Squadron, Fourth Fighter Group, which was the Eight Air Force in Europe. The unit destroyed over one thousand German aircraft by war's end. Gentile has the record for "bagging" (i.e. shooting down) the most planes when he shot down 30 German airplanes during WWII.

Don Gentile made his last flight in 1951. He was piloting a two-seat, T-33 trainer, which crashed due to engine failure, killing him and a passenger. He was honored with a posthumous promotion to Major. His decorations include the Distinguished Service Cross, the Silver Star, the Distinguished Flying Cross, the British Distinguished Flying Cross, and the British Star. He was also posthumously inducted into the Aviation Hall of Fame.

Charles Bonaparte

Still others chose another form of serve to their country. Take Charles Bonaparte as an example. Charles Bonaparte chose to dedicate a good part of his life working within the Federal Government to "level the playing field" between big business monopolies or special interest groups and the average citizens.

Charles Bonaparte was born in Baltimore, Maryland on June 9, 1851. He received his law degree from Harvard University. In 1908, President Theodore Roosevelt appointed him the 46th Attorney General of the United States. He soon discovered that he was hampered with his charge of carrying out President Roosevelt's "trust-busting" policies because he lacked the investigative staff necessary.

On July 28, 1908, Bonaparte issued the order, which made the special investigative force a permanent subdivision of the Department of Justice. In 1935, what had begun as a 23 man unit under Bonaparte's direction was renamed the *Federal Bureau of Investigation.* In addition for his work as the Attorney General of the United States, Bonaparte is also remembered as the founder the National Civil Service Reform League, and as an organizer and president of the National Municipal League. He was also a member of the Indian tribal commission and the Secretary of the Navy.

He argued over 50 Supreme Court cases and led the Department of Justice in pursuing landmark antitrust investigations involving the Standard Oil Company, the American Tobacco Company, and the Union Pacific Railroad. He accomplished all of this when there was a prejudice in this country against Italians. For example, in 1906, the same year that Bonaparte was appointed Attorney General, the United States paid indemnity to Italy because of the failure of New Orleans officials to prevent the mass lynching of Italian citizens. Bonaparte believed in active citizens. He fought for the right of individual citizens against the special interest. When people told him that he could not win against the big monopolies, he reminded them of what another Italian, Dante, had said a few centuries earlier:

"The hottest places in hell were reserved for those in time of moral crisis preserve their neutrality"

The Italian Historical Society of America has held an annual ceremony in his honor at the Department of Justice for the last forty years.

Mario Cuomo

Mario Cuomo is another interesting example of a person from Italian immigrant family roots who decided to dedicate his life to government service.

Mario Cuomo was the first Italian-American governor of New York. He drew national attention in the 1980s as a gifted and inspiring political speaker of this generation.

Cuomo was born in 1932 in a room above the family grocery store in the New York neighborhood of South Jamaica, Queens. His parents were immigrants who had arrived in the United States just a few years earlier from Southern Italy. His early background included a fling with a minor league baseball team. His early political ventures were unsuccessful. As an example, he lost to Edward Koch in the 1977 race for the Mayor of New York City. But in 1982, his competitive nature and his desire to serve propelled him to win the election for governor over the heavily favored Koch.

Cuomo won his second term by the greatest margin in the history of New York gubernatorial races. He is a deeply religious Catholic and family man. Cuomo remained so formidable in 1990 that, despite a bad economy and massive budget problems, the Republicans had difficulty finding anyone to run against him and many had him on the top of the list of Democratic Presidential prospects.

Rudy Giuliani

He is sometimes called "a priest in pinstripes" because he was always thought of by many as a tough lawyer, prosecutor, but always on the side of righteousness. But in the tragedy that occurred on September 11, 2001, New York City Mayor Rudolph Giuliani as David Letterman stated, "is the personification of what courage is". Know for his hard edged politics and "love it or leave it" attitude for those who complained about New York, Mayor Giuliani suddenly seems very composed, very mellow, but much focused. Without once even flinching it seems, he swung into action to get New York back on his feet.

Almost 2 months to the date, another American Airlines passenger jet goes down over a heavily populated area of Queens's carrying 252 people, crew included. A CNN reporter notes that Rudolph Giuliani is on the scene "Cool, calm and collective as usual. In 1944, Rudolph W. Giuliani was born to a working class family in Brooklyn, New York. As the grandson of Italian immigrants, Mayor Giuliani learned a strong work ethic and a deep respect for America's ideal of equal opportunity.

He attended Bishop Loughlin Memorial High School (Class of '61) in Brooklyn, Manhattan College (Class of '65) in the Bronx and New York University Law School in Manhattan, graduating magna cum laude in 1968. Upon graduation, Rudy Giuliani clerked for Judge Lloyd MacMahon, United States District Judge for the Southern District of New York. In 1970, Giuliani joined the office of the U.S. Attorney. At age 29, he was named Chief of the Narcotics Unit and rose to serve as executive US Attorney. In 1975, Giuliani was recruited to Washington, D.C., where he was named Associate Deputy Attorney General and chief of staff to the Deputy Attorney General. From 1977 to 1981, Giuliani returned to New York to practice law at Patterson, Belknap, Webb and Tyler.

In 1981, Giuliani was named Associate Attorney General, the third highest position in the Department of Justice. As Associate Attorney General, Giuliani supervised all of the US Attorney Offices' Federal law enforcement agencies, the Bureau of Corrections, the Drug Enforcement Agency, and the US Marshals. In 1983, Giuliani was appointed US Attorney for the Southern District of New York. There, he spearheaded the effort to jail drug dealers, fight organized crime, break the web of corruption in government, and prosecute white-collar criminals.

Few US Attorneys in history can match his record of 4,152 convictions with only 25 reversals.

In 1989, Giuliani entered the race for mayor of New York City as a candidate of the Republican and Liberal parties, losing by the closest margin in City history. However in 1993, his campaign focusing on quality of life, crime, business and education made him the 107th Mayor of the City of New York. In 1997 he was re-elected by a wide margin, carrying four out of New York City's five boroughs.

As Mayor, Rudy Giuliani returned accountability to City government and improved the quality of life to New Yorkers. Overall crime was down 57%, murder was reduced 65%, and New York City—once infamous around the world for its dangerous streets—was recognized by the F.B.I. as the safest large city in America for the past five years. Under his leadership, New York City became the best-known example of the resurgence of urban America.

Louis Freeh

Louis Freeh is an excellent example of an Italian-American servant dedicated to public service. Louis was born in Jersey City, New Jersey. He graduated Phi Beta Kappa from Rutgers College in 1971 and received his law degree from Rutgers Law School in 1974 and an LL.M. degree in criminal law from New York University Law School in 1984. He also served as a First Lieutenant in the United States Army Reserve.

Other positions held by Louis Freeh included FBI Special Agent from 1975 to 1981 in the New York City Field Office and at FBI Headquarters in Washington D.C. He was also Assistant United States Attorney in the Southern District of New York starting in 1981 where he held the positions there as Chief of the Organized Crime Unit, Deputy United States Attorney, and Associate United States Attorney.

In July 1991 former President George Bush appointed Freeh as United States District Court Judge for the Southern District of New York. While serving in this position, he was nominated to be the Director of the FBI by President Clinton on July 20, 1993. He was confirmed by the Senate on August 6, 1993 and sworn in as Director on September 1, 1993. For his service, Freeh has received a number of honors including the Attorney General's Award for Distinguish Service, the John Marshal Award for Preparation of Litigation, Ethics in Government Award, and the Federal Law Enforcement Officers Association Award.

Sonny Bono

Sonny Bono gave up a very profitable career in the entertainment industry to enter government service. Sonny was born on February 16, 1935 in Detroit Michigan. His father, Santo was a truck driver and his mother Jean was a beautician. He was raised a Roman Catholic and attended Inglewood High School but he dropped out in 1952. He became famous as a musician and one half of the *Sonny and Cher* team, which included a long running television show. He also acted in a number of films including *Hairspray, Airplane II,* and *Escape to Athena.*

While Cher continued her acting and singing career, Sonny gave up the money to enter politics and was elected Mayor of Palm Springs, CA. in 1988. He was elected to the United States Congress from the 44th District, from 1995 until his death in 1998. His wife, Mary Bono, replaced him in his House seat. Sonny Bono died on January 5, 1998 in an accident at Heavenly Valley Ski Resort, CA.

In Cher's eulogy for Sonny, she said, "there was a section in *Reader's Digest.* It was called "The Most Unforgettable Character I've ever met". And for me that was Sonny Bono. And no matter how long I live or who I meet in my life, that person will always be Sonny for me."

Albert Sacco

Albert Sacco had his dream come true and provided a valuable service to his country at the same time. Albert Sacco was an astronaut and flew as a payload specialist on STS-73, which launched on October 20, 1995. It landed at the Kennedy Space Center on November 5, 1995. The 16 day mission aboard Columbia focused on materials science, biotechnology, combustion science, and fluid physics contained within the Spacelab module.

Albert Sacco was born on May 3, 1949 into an Italian family in Boston Massachusetts. He graduated from Belmont Senior High School in 1968 and received his Bachelor of Science degree in Chemical Engineering with honors from Northeastern University in Boston in 1973. He was awarded a Doctorate in

Chemical Engineering from the Massachusetts Institute of Technology in Cambridge in 1977.

Since 1977, Professor Sacco has been on the faculty at the Worcester Polytechnic Institute in the Department of Chemical Engineering. He splits his time between research and teaching. He was appointed department head in 1989. Along with his father Al Sr. and his brother Bernard, in his spare time, he ran a family restaurant in Boston for over twenty years. Albert received the Admiral Earl Award, given by the Worcester Engineering Society, for meritorious contributions in applied sciences, specifically in the fields of catalysis and absorbent deactivation. He also received a National Science Foundation Young Faculty Initiation Grant in 1978.

NY Italian-American Fire Fighters, Police and other Rescue Workers on 9-11-01

In addition to the people mentioned above, I would also like to make a special point and mention the Italian-Americans who were killed in the tragedy on September 11, 2001. There were a number of heroic Italian-Americas that gave their lives assisting others during the 9-11-01 disaster in New York City. A review of the list of fatalities shows that the Italian-America community took more then its' share of the fatalities in the collapse of those two buildings. A number of Italian-American rescue workers lost their lives in the effort to save lives. Some of those rescue workers that lost their lives include:

Chief Pete Ganci, who held the title chief of fire department, had been working his multichannel radio, standing at the center of the smoky chaos in front of 1 World Trade Center on Tuesday and personally commanding the rescue efforts when the building collapsed. He and the mayor had spoken only minutes before.

John P. Napolitano who won enough awards, medals and citations from the New York Fire Department and the Lakeland Fire District in Ronkonkoma, N.Y., in his career to weigh down his chest.

Gerard Barbara who was assistant chief of the New York Fire Department Mr. Barbara, 53, was a 31-year veteran of the Fire Department, one of the city's highest-ranking supervisors. He was walking toward the lobby of the second trade center tower when the building collapsed.

All the people in this section are just examples of the many Italian-Americans who have served the United States with honor and distinction over the last two hundred years. Many of them have made the ultimate sacrifice but many have made other deep sacrifices as well. Our community should be proud of their accomplishments.

15

The Value of Preserving Your Heritage

Our forefathers had the deepest respect for our traditions and our heritage. They celebrated it every chance that they had. They were poor but they were rich in their culture and their history and they knew it. They shared their culture with each new generation as a rich and precious asset. My parents passed this deep respect for my heritage and traditions on to me as well. I know that many of the other Italian-American parents did so as well. You can see this by the number of Italian-American organizations that are thriving in the United States today. Each of these organizations is dedicated to the preservation and education of the Italian culture and traditions.

In this section, we will introduce you to some of these Italian-American organizations that are addressing their specific needs and maintaining the rich culture and traditions of our forefathers.

We will also discuss some of the large number of annual Italian-American festivals that take place each year in the United States. It is a significant number and the crowds get bigger each year as the festivals get more popular. In my research, it may be yet another sign of the resurgence toward a desire to "return to your Italian roots"

Let's discuss some of the Italian-American festivals first.

ANNUAL ITALIAN-AMERICAN FESTIVALS

Italian festivals are a great way to have fun and they invite the full community to participate. People come together and reunite in their old neighborhoods to share

189

their history and the values, which unite them. In today's multicultural society, an Italian festival recognizes and displays its own distinctiveness through its celebrations. Many people work very hard in both preparation and in participating to make these festivals a success. As Italians became more established in their neighborhoods, they became more integrated into these local celebrations.

Listed below are some examples of festivals that are produced each year in the United States.

Columbus Day Parades

Columbus Day was first celebrated on October 12, 1792 to honor the day Christopher Columbus landed in the Bahamas in 1492. President Benjamin Harrison celebrated it again one hundred years later. The celebration of Columbus Day was begun by Italian immigrants in New York in 1866. Other communities followed suit, and three years later the Italians in San Francisco held a celebration on October 12th, and called it Columbus Day. Since 1920, it has been celebrated annually and, in 1971, became a federal legal holiday to be celebrated on the second Monday in October.

In 1937 President Franklin Delano Roosevelt declared the day a national holiday. Although there has been much opposition to the holiday in recent years, many Italian-Americans take this holiday as an opportunity to celebrate Italian-American culture and heritage. The traditional Columbus Day in the United States includes a parade down New York's Fifth Avenue. Parades and pageantry are often featured in many towns and cities across the United States.

On Columbus Day it was a tradition in our neighborhood to have a Spaghettata (a spaghetti dinner). This has been held at the St. Gabriel's Church. The priest there was Italian, and let the community have use of the space and the kitchen.

New York's Annual Feast of San Gennaro

Presented annually since 1996 by Figli di San Gennaro, Inc., a not-for-profit organization, this year's Feast will again bring more than 1 million people to the streets of Little Italy in the annual salute to the Patron Saint of Naples. The street festivities—including parades, entertainment, food stands and a cannoli-eating contest—are capped on September 19th with a celebratory Mass and candlelit procession as the Statue of the Saint is carried from its permanent home in Most Precious Blood Church on Mulberry Street.

Festa Italiana Association of Portland

Each year a celebration is held with the primary objective (according to its' promoters) is "to promote Italian culture throughout the Greater Portland Community, to provide an opportunity for people, Italian-American and non Italian-American alike, to come together to celebrate the unique and profound contributions of Italy and her sons and daughters to the thought, art, and science of the Western World throughout the centuries."

The celebration is held in the later part of August beginning, like all Italian festivals, with a celebratory Mass. The mass is celebrated in Italian on the Saturday night proceeding the week of activities in Pioneer Courthouse Square. The next day, Sunday, is the Invitational Bocce Tournament, which over the past several years has been held at Italian-owned Ponzi Vineyards

Other events may follow during the early part of "Festa" week, such as: "Festa night at the Flicks" featuring a well known and popular Italian film, a cooking demonstration in downtown Portland, or a "Celebration of Italian Heritage" to include lectures, Italian readings, piano and musical interludes and Italian art displays...

On Thursday night Pioneer Courthouse Square becomes "Piazza Italia" throughout the weekend and culminating on Sunday evening. A piazza is the focus of every Italian village, and such will be the case at Festa Italiana. "A Concert in the Piazza" comes alive on Thursday night with local opera musicians performing arias and ensembles from Italian operas.

Wisconsin's Festa Italiana

The first Festa Italiana, was 90 years ago in front of Our Lady of Pompeii Church, the first Italian national church in Wisconsin. It was sponsored by a group of the city's first Italian immigrants from the Sicilian town of Santo Stefano de Camastra. In early September of 1906, they honored their patron, the

Holy Crucifix, with a two-day celebration—a tradition which had been carried on for centuries in their native hometown.

The festival included a traditional religious procession, in which the effigy of the Holy Crucifix was carried through the streets. There was also a traditional brass band playing Italian marches and selections from Italian composers as Verdi, Puccini and Mascagni. There were also fireworks displays and many of them attending their first festival tasted those traditional Italian dishes so familiar to Italians families including homemade sausage and frying green peppers.

For more than 60 years, the immigrants of Santo Stefano di Camastra, along with three other Italian immigrant groups, held weekend festivals in the city during the summer to honor their respective hometown saints.

In June, the festival of St. Joseph was sponsored by the immigrants of Bagheria. Those from Porticello, Sicily, honored their patroness, La Madonna del Lume, in July. In August, immigrants from the Adriatic regions of Italy paid homage to St. Rocco. The previously mentioned Holy Crucifix Society festival was staged annually on the second weekend in September. The only time all four festivals were suspended was during the World Wars. During those years, only the religious procession took place.

Cleveland's Feast of the Assumption

More than 100,000 Clevelanders flock to Little Italy for a four-day celebration of the Feast of the Assumption each August to celebrate the Assumption of Mary, mother of Jesus, rose into heaven. The crowds pack the pews of Holy Rosary Church for the Aug. 15 Mass. They honor Mary as she's carried down the street by the parishioners; accompanied by smiling young girls in lacy First Communion dresses. And they take in traditional Italian bands on the street.

The festival in Little Italy shows, they haven't forgotten their roots. The 2000 census counted 177,310 Italian-Americans in metropolitan Cleveland. Though there's little new immigration from Italy, this is more than a 14 percent increase from 1990, a sign more third- and fourth-generation Italians are beginning to embrace their roots

San Diego Festa

As of the writing of this book, San Diego's Little Italy experienced its largest Annual Festa ever on October 10th. 2004. The Fourth Annual Little Italy Precious Festa estimated, "a minimum of 90,000 people to the streets of Little Italy for this one day event. Since its inception in 1995, San Diego's Little Italy Festa has grown from a one block event into one that spans over 15 square blocks and tens of thousands of visitors.

Ferragosto in the Bronx

Each year the neighborhood holds a festival called Ferragosto. Ferragosto, or the "Feast that Begins in August," has its roots in Roman harvest festivals. Peasants that earned the lands of Roman patricians (elite class) would celebrate the end of the summer harvest by honoring the Gods of agriculture. They formally visited the house of their patron, who gave them presents, often money. This is one of the earliest examples of "tipping" or La mance. Today, Ferragosto is usually held on August 15. Ferragosto is an opportunity for family and paisanes (neighbors) to enjoy the sun, good company and of course, good food.

A list of annual Italian-American festivals is at the end of this Chapter.

HERITAGE ORGANIZATIONS

Order of the Sons of Italy in America

Today's Order of the Sons of Italy in America has a few missions including encouraging the study of Italian language and culture in America schools and universities; preserving Italian American traditions, culture, history, and heritage, and promote good relationships between the United States and Italy.

OSIA researches Italian American culture and history, promotes the study of Italian in the United States, and encourages young Italian Americans through scholarships and educational programs as well as organizing grassroots legislative efforts on issues important to Italian Americans.

The Order also manages *The Sons of Italy Foundation (SIF)*, which is a private, philanthropic institution established by OSIA. Since its' founding, the Foundation has given more then $83 million to scholarships, medical research, cultural preservation, and other projects.

The Commission for Social Justice is the anti-defamation arm of the OSIA. The CSJ serves to protect against racism, prejudice, and the stereotyping of all races, religions and cultures.

The Campanian Society

The Campanian Society is a non-profit organization dedicated to the advancement of knowledge in the humanities and in fine arts and in the social and cultural history of Naples and Campania. The Society sponsors activities and programs in classical humanities, Greek and Roman social History, fine arts and architecture. The Society also produces comprehensive educational material in various subjects that include ready to use teaching packages for teachers across elementary, middle and high school curriculum.

The Campanian Society Tour Programs take educators and travelers into the world of classical tradition of literature, theater arts, sculpture and painting through the ages. The Society also provides travel programs for the blind and visually impaired and custom programs for teachers and students as well.

National Italian-American Foundation

The National Italian American Foundation (NIAF) was founded in 1975, as a non-profit, non-partisan organization in Washington D.C. NIAF is the major advocate for the nearly 25 million Italian American in the United States. Its mission is to preserve and to protect Italian American heritage and culture through its programs.

One of its programs is Italian American Heritage Month. To celebrate Italian American Heritage Month, NIAF offers a series of free Italian languages courses and free walking tours of Italian American neighborhoods in a total of eight cities across the United States. The cities in this program are San Francisco, St. Louis, Chicago, Pittsburgh, Philadelphia, Boston, New York, and Washington. The celebration last the entire month of October.

Another of its programs is the Italian Language & Culture Teacher of the Year Award. One of NIAF's top priorities is to promote the Italian language in the United States. Beginning in 2003, NIAF, started honoring a teacher for excellence in Italian language and culture in classroom education. NIAF also offers the *Italian4US* Course Package produced by Italian Culture on the Net, a consortium of 24 Italian Universities aimed at electronically promoting language, culture, and image of Italy all over the world.

It provides grants in Italian language study, culture and heritage, and to college and university clubs. And it also has a very active scholarship program, *The National Italian American Foundation,* which has an annual education budget of $1,000,000 for deserving students. Each October, NIAF holds its' Annual Convention in Washington, D.C. It is the largest formal gathering of Italian Americans in the United States. Its Convention includes an Anniversary Gala Dinner, honoring outstanding Italian Americans in business, science, sports entertainment, and philanthropy. The dinner draws more than 3,000 people each year and has been attended by five sitting United States Presidents.

FIERI

FIERI International is a club for young Italian-Americans. It was founded in 1984 by two Italian-American College Club Presidents—John Calvelli of Fordham University and Gina Biancardi of Lehman College both of the Bronx in New York City. They first met to discuss the possibility of sponsoring events together. But in time, it grew to a much bigger need to unite young Italian-American students and professionals beyond the confines of a college campus.

It started as the Belmont Italian-American Cultural Association and held local events spearheaded by Cavelli but within months, the demand grew throughout the New York metropolitan area. Their new name became "Fiere International". This came from a song were the word fiere (proud) was mentioned repeatedly with the singer's pride in being Italian. It was perfect for the members of the club so the new name was accepted.

The goals of the club are to preserve the Italian culture, encourage the study of the Italian language and history, and foster the value of higher education and personal achievement in Italian men and women. Chapters are growing very quickly as this book is being written. New chapters are in the works in places such as Long Island, Milwaukee, Philadelphia, San Diego, Stamford, Los Angeles, and Florida.

The Italian-American Institute of Township of Ocean, New Jersey

Italian-American Institute of the Township of Ocean, New Jersey is dedicated to remembering the heritage and culture of the Italian traditions and culture in the Township. It began about 30 years ago with a few dedicated members and now has over 350 members in their group. They recently purchased a new Italian Cultural Center, which serves as their headquarters. They provide weekly Italian language classes, a wide choice of classes for adults in Italian Culture at Brookdale College, and thousands of dollars in scholarships are given annually to deserving local students that pursue Italian Studies.

Over 80,000 people attended their latest four day Annual Italian Festival and enjoyed the great traditional Italian food and fun.

Order Italian Sons and Daughters of America

The Order Italian Sons and Daughters of America (ISDA) was founded to perpetuate Italian American culture and values by sponsoring social, civic, and cultural events and programs. ISDA was founded in 1930 and currently has over 120 lodges throughout the United States.

The ISDA Fraternal Association provides social contacts and charitable activities through its' lodges in Pennsylvania, Ohio, West Virginia, New York, Michigan, Florida, California, Illinois, and Indiana. In addition to there monthly meetings, the social activities at each lodge could include bowling leagues, golf, bocce, "pot luck dinners" and dances. Annual events could include the "Italian Day Outing", the "Debutante Ball", the "Annual Christmas Party", and "The Columbus Day Parade".

A Scholarship Fund was established in 1969 to provide financial assistance to youth members attending accredited colleges and universities. The Association also provided a variety of insurance products to it's' members.

Italia Unita

Italia Unita Organization is a non-profit organization that celebrates Italian culture. It was founded in 1995 and is still an entirely volunteer effort. The signature project of Italia Unita is the Italian Festival held in East Boston each year. Italia Unita was started as a festival in 1995.

A few of East Boston's Italians were celebrating Italy in the World Cup and some impromptu celebrations erupted and a few people noticed and decided to organize a three-day festive of Italian pride. The word spread and people who were previously linked to East Boston started returning to celebrate also. This festival has become very popular among second and third generation Italian-Americans. Ten years later, it is one of the largest Italian festivals in the United States with visitors from all over the world The team continues to offer other cultural services to their community including "Strictly Sinatra Night" and Italian classes. They are on their way to support their community in keeping their Italian culture alive and well.

National Organization of Italian American Women

The National Organization of Italian American Women (NOIA) was founded in 1980 by a small group of Italian American women. They wanted to develop a national network for Italian-American women and create aspirations of its members and to combat ethnic stereotypes by promoting positive role models. Their membership is comprised of a diverse group of women from varied professional backgrounds as well as homemakers. It is the only national membership organization for women of Italian ancestry.

The NOIAW holds seven to ten meetings a year on issues of interest to Italian American women. Programs include a mentoring program for students in undergraduate and graduate programs; and they annually award scholarships to deserving students to help them achieve their career goals. The Mentor Program matches a NOIAW member with young women interested in and/or pursuing a career in the Mentor's field. The NOIAW Mentor Program was the very first such program within the Italian American community. Begun in 1983, it joined NIAF's Program in 1988, and Mentoring USA in 1996.

The NOIAW is also is committed to preserving Italian heritage, language, and culture while simultaneously promoting and supporting the advancement of women of Italian American ancestry. NOIAW has established international links with women of Italian ancestry in other countries and have held many international conferences in New York, Italy, Argentina & Australia

Italian Heritage Society

The Italian Heritage Society is dedicated to both the preservation and advancement of the Italian culture in Michigan. The heart of Italian Culture beats strongly in the State of Michigan. The Italian Heritage Society is an outgrowth of the Italian Heritage Room located at Wayne State University in Detroit, Michigan. Heritage Room Benefactors, Donors, Contributors and Sponsors worked together to form this organization to manage the future of the Heritage Room.

Since this time, the organization has grown to support the furtherance of Italian culture, both abroad and at home. All fund-raising proceeds benefit the creation of the Italian Heritage Society Endowment Fund to establish a Professorship / Endowed Chair in Italian Studies and Research at Wayne State University.

ITALIAN FESTIVALS

STATE	CITY	FESTA & DATE
California	Belmont Shore	So Cal Italian Festival AUTUMN www.SOCALitalianFESTIVAL.com
California	Lodi	Festa Italiana JUNE
California	Los Angeles	The Feast of San Gennaro Festival SEPTEMBER www.Feastofla.org
California	Oakland, Jack London Square	Festa SEPTEMBER

STATE	CITY	FESTA & DATE
California	Redwood City	Columbus Day Italian American Heritage Celebration OCTOBER
California	Sacramento	Italian Festival first weekend of AUGUST www.italiancenter.net
California	San Diego	Little Italy Festa OCTOBER www.littleitalysd.com
California	San Francisco	North American Trentino Convention July 1-4, 2004 www.trentino-sanfrancisco.com
California	San Jose	Italian Family Festival OCTOBER
California	San Mateo	Festa Italiana JULY
California	Santa Barbara, Oak Park	Italian Festa OCTOBER
California	San Francisco	Feste of the Madonna del Lume SEPTEMBER
California	San Rafael	The Italian Film Festival 6 Saturdays in October & November
California	Santa Rosa	Festa Italiana SEPTEMBER
California	Visalia	Putignano-Visalia Sister City Italian Festival OCTOBER
Colorado	Denver	Feast of St. Rocco AUGUST
Connecticut	Ansonia	Italian Festa AUGUST
Connecticut	New Haven	St. Andrew Apostle Society's 104th Annual Italian Feast JUNE

STATE	CITY	FESTA & DATE
Connecticut	New Haven	Feast of St. Anthony JUNE
Connecticut	Norwich	The Taste of Italy SEPTEMBER
Connecticut	Stratford	Italian Picnic AUGUST
Connecticut	Waterbury	Lady of Mount Carmel Festival JULY
Connecticut	Waterbury	San Donato Festa AUGUST
Connecticut	Westport	Festival Italiano JULY
Delaware	Wilmington	St Anthony's Italian American Festival JUNE
Florida	Delray Beach	Columbus Day Italian Festa OCTOBER
Florida	Ft. Walton Beach	Festa Italiana Columbus Day Weekend OCTOBER
Florida	Palm Coast	Festa OCTOBER http://members.pcfl.net/iasc
Florida	Tampa	Festa Italiana APRIL http://www.festaitalianatampa.com
Florida	Tampa	St. Joseph Feast MARCH http://www.italian-club.org
Florida	Venice	Italian Feast and Carnival FEBRUARY
Florida	Vero Beach	Italian Food Festival MARCH

STATE	CITY	FESTA & DATE
Florida	Vero Beach	Columbus Day Fest OCTOBER
Georgia	Atlanta	La Dolce Vita MAY www.abrauction2002.com
Illinois	Benld	Italian American Days MAY
Illinois	Berwyn	Maria Santissima Lauretana di Altavilla Milicia SEPTEMBER
Illinois	Blue Island	Feast of St. Donatus AUGUST
Illinois	Chicago Heights	Feast of St. Lorenzo AUGUST
Illinois	Chicago	Heart of Italy Food & Wine Festival JUNE
Illinois	Chicago, North Lake	Villa Day SEPTEMBER St.Joseph MARCH
Illinois	Chicago	Fieri National Convention May
Illinois	Chicago	Societa San Giovanni Bosco Di Ciminna JULY
Illinois	Farmington	Italian Festa SEPTEMBER
Illinois	Melrose Park	Our Lady of Mt Carmel Festival JULY
Illinois	Rockford	Festa Italiana AUGUST
Illinois	Springfield	Ethnic Festival SEPTEMBER
Illinois	Stone Park	Italian Day Picnic AUGUST

STATE	CITY	FESTA & DATE
Illinois	Stone Park	Feast of St. Beato Giovanni Liccio di Caccamo MAY
Illinois	Stone Park	Feast of St. Francesco di Paola AUGUST
Iowa	Des Moines	Festa Italiana AUGUST
Louisiana	Harvey	St. Rosalie Parish Fair SEPTEMBER
Louisiana	New Orleans	Maria Santissima Della Favara Feast SEPTEMBER
Maine	Portland	Feast of Assumption & St. Rocco's Street Bazaar AUGUST
Maryland	Baltimore	Feast of St. Anthony JUNE
Maryland	Baltimore	Feast of San Gabriel AUGUST
Massachusetts	North Adams	JuneFest, Italian Street Fair JUNE
Massachusetts	Boston	Italia Unita JULY www.italiaunita.org
Massachusetts	Boston	Madonna Del Grazie JULY
Massachusetts	Boston	Madonna Della Cava Festival AUGUST
Massachusetts	Boston	Madonna del Soccorso AUGUST www.fishermansfeast.com
Massachusetts	Cambridge	Feast of Saints Cosmas and Damian SEPTEMBER www.cosmas-and-damian.com
Massachusetts	East Boston	Italia Unita Italian Festival JULY

STATE	CITY	FESTA & DATE
Massachusetts	North Boston	St. Anthony's Feast AUGUST Feast of St. Lucy AUGUST
Massachusetts	Lawrence	Feast of the Three Saints Labor Day AUGUST & SEPTEMBER
Massachusetts	Worcester	Feast of Our Lady of Mount Carmel JULY
Michigan	Grand Rapids	Festa Italiana AUGUST
Michigan	Sterling Heights	Italian Festival at Freedom Hill Park JULY
Minnesota	Chisholm	Festa Italiana JULY www.ironworld.com
Missouri	Saint Louis	Columbus Day Parade and Festival OCTOBER
Nebraska	Omaha	La Festa Italiana Labor Day Weekend SEPTEMBER
Nevada	Las Vegas	San Gennaro SEPTEMBER
Nevada	Reno	Eldorado's Italian Festival OCTOBER www.eldoradoreno.com
New Jersey	Bayonne	Italian Carnival AUGUST
New Jersey	Hammonton	Feast of Mt.Carmel JULY
New Jersey	Hoboken	St. Ann's Italian Festival JULY
New Jersey	Hoboken	Feast of the Madonna del Martiri SEPTEMBER

STATE	CITY	FESTA & DATE
New Jersey	No. Wildwood	Elks Italian American Weekend JUNE
New Jersey	Oakhurst	Italian American Festival AUGUST
New Jersey	West Windsor, Mercer County	SEPTEMBER www.italianamericanfestival.com
New York	Bronx	St. Anthony Feast JUNE Mt Carmel Feast JULY www.MtCarmelFeasts.com
New York	Brooklyn	Feast of the Giglio JULY
New York	Glen Cove	Feast of St. Rocco JULY–AUGUST
New York	Glen Cove	Tomato Festival AUGUST
New York	Hempstead, Hof- stra University	Italian Festival SEPTEMBER
New York	Manhattan	San Gennaro Festival SEPTEMBER
New York	Mechanicville	Feast of the Assumption AUGUST
New York	New York	San Gandolfo Feast JUNE
New York	Oyster Bay (Long Island)	St. Rocco Festival JULY
New York	PoughKeepsie	Festa Italiana SEPTEMBER www.theitaliancenter.com
New York	Scotia	Capital Region Festa Italiana AUGUST
New York	Syracuse	Festa Italiana SEPTEMBER

STATE	CITY	FESTA & DATE
New York	Utica	Festival of Saints Cosmos and Damian SEPTEMBER
New York	Watertown	Mt. Carmel Italian Religious Festival
New York	Watertown	Bravo Italiano Festival SEPTEMBER
New York	West Harrison	St. Anthony of Padua Church Festa Italiana JUNE
New York	White Plains	Our Lady of Mount Caramel Church Festa Italiana JULY
New York	Valhalla	Italian Festival JULY
Ohio	Candied (Young-stown)	Youngstown Italian Festival JULY
Ohio	Canton	Italian American Festival JUNE
Ohio	Columbus	St. John's Italian Festival SEPTEMBER
Ohio	Lowellville	Our Lady of Mt. Carmel Festa JULY
Ohio	Niles	Italian-American Festival JULY
Oklahoma	McAlester, S.E. Expo Complex	Italian Festival MAY
Oregon	Portland	Festa Italiana AUGUST www.festa-italiana.org
Pennsylvania	Alquippa	Festa di San Rocco AUGUST
Pennsylvania	Crabtree	Feast of Our Lady of Mt. Carmel JULY
Pennsylvania	Dunmore	Italian Festival AUGUST

STATE	CITY	FESTA & DATE
Pennsylvania	Edensberg	Italian Musical MAY
Pennsylvania	Easton	Tempo Italiano
Pennsylvania	Erie	St. Joseph's Day Celebration MARCH
Pennsylvania	Erie	1. St. Paul's Festival of the Assumption AUGUST 2. Mazzini Civic Ass. Italian American Picnic JULY
Pennsylvania	Norristown	Our Lady of Mount Caramel Festival JULY
Pennsylvania	Norristown	Maria Santissima del Soccorso di Sciacca Festa AUGUST
Pennsylvania	Norristown	Santissimo Salvatore di Montella Festival AUGUST
Pennsylvania	Old Forge	Felittese Festival SEPTEMBER
Pennsylvania	Philadelphia	Feast of St. Anthony Di Padova JUNE 4
Pennsylvania	Pittsburgh	Festa Italia OCTOBER
Pennsylvania	Scranton	Italian Festival SEPTEMBER
Rhode Island	Newport	Festa Italiana OCTOBER
Rhode Island	Westerly	Mount Carmel Feast JULY
Tennessee	Memphis	Memphis Italian Festival 1st weekend in JUNE
Tennessee	Nashville	Italian Street Fair SEPTEMBER www.nashvillecitysearch.com/italianfair

STATE	CITY	FESTA & DATE
Texas	Houston	Festa Italiana SEPTEMBER www.houstonitalianfestival.com
Virginia	Bluefield	OSIA Italian Festival first weekend in OCTOBER
Virginia	Richmond	Viva Italia JULY
Washington	Seattle	Italian Festival SEPTEMBER www.festaseattle.com
Washington	Walla Walla	Italian Heritage Days Festa & Parade OCTOBER
Washington, District of Columbia		Festa Italiana OCTOBER
West Virginia	Bluefield	OSIA Italian Festival first weekend in October
West Virginia	Clarksburg	Annual Italian Heritage Festival AUGUST SEPTEMBER
West Virginia	Wheeling	Upper Ohio Valley Italian Festival JULY www.italyfest.com
Wisconsin	Kenosha	Feast of Our Lady of the Holy Rosary AUGUST
Wisconsin	Kenosha	Our Lady of Mt. Carmel Festival JULY
Wisconsin	Madison	Festa Italiana JUNE www.iwcmadison.org/2001festa.html
Wisconsin	Milwaukee	Festa Italiana JULY www.festaitaliana.com

STATE	CITY	FESTA & DATE
Wisconsin	Racine	Roma Lodge
		JULY

NIAF Research Department
1860–19th Street, NW
Washington, DC 20009

16

The Value in Investing in Continuing Educational & Professional Activities

Initially, the Italian immigrant was focused on their children working as early as possible to help the family survive in this new land rather then getting an education. However, by the second generation, when the basic necessities were assured in most households, the family refocused their efforts and realized the importance of a quality of education for their children.

From my earliest memories, my mother told me how important it was to go to college and get a good education. Each family in the neighborhood had dreams for their children to grow up to be doctors, lawyers, engineers, or to get business degrees so that they may be able to expand the family business. As time went by and these dreams were realized, Italian-Americans also banded together to form organization to help them advance in their careers or to expand their knowledge in a given area of expertise.

In this section of the book, we will explore some of those organizations and discuss their history and how they help Italian-Americans advance in their careers or assist in their education.

EDUCATIONAL ORGANIZATIONS

John D. Calandra Italian American Institute

The John D. Calandra Italian American Institute at the City University of New York was founded to foster higher education among Italian-Americans. It is the only research institute devoted to the study of Italian-Americans. The birth of the Institute came in 1979 and was the direct response to several factors taking place within City University of New York (CUNY) at that time.

First, there was a significant increase in new students entering CUNY from diverse ethnic groups, including many Italians. Also, Dr. Richard Bossone, then President of the Association of Italian American faculty at CUNY met with the Chancellor, Robert Kibbee, expressing his concerns about perceived issues of discrimination. When Dr. Bossone met with Italian-American students about their concerns, the result was a joint report: *Italian Americans: The Neglected Minority in the City University of New York.*

Although some things at the University did change for the better, advocates continued to press the issue and under the leadership of New York Senator John Calandra, legislative hearings were conducted. As a result, specific recommendations were made that an Institute for Italian Americans be established at CUNY to provide the academic community with guidance, cultural, and international services. Senator Calandra had laid the groundwork for the creation of the Institute.

On September 13, 1979, the Italian American Institute to Foster Higher Education was incorporated as a non-profit corporation with Rev. Fr. Nicholas Russo, Ph. D. as Executive Director. The Institute's objectives were to serve as the center for sociological, political, and historical data; provide a central clearing house to disseminate information of interest to all Italophiles; to coordinate a counseling program with special emphasis on career guidance; to develop a research institute to study the Italian American experience in an urban academic community; to encourage Italian Americans students to participate in student government; to create a library, resources, media center, and informational programs pertaining to the Italian American experience; and to establish a Speakers Bureau at CUNY.

With the exception of a brief period in time, the Institute has done quite well in its history. There was a time in 1984 when money was tight and the Institute had to be restructured under the able leadership of Joseph Scelsa, Ed.D. In 1986, Senator John Calandra died and in 1987 the Institute was renamed in his honor. In 1994, the Institute officially joined with the other ethic areas of studies at Queens College in a signing ceremony on October 17.

PROFESSIONAL INDIVIDUALS/ORGANIZATIONS

Rinaldo Brutocao

Rinaldo Brutocao is a well known international executive, writer and speaker. He is widely recognized as a practical visionary, change agent and futurist. Rinaldo is Co-founder and President of the World Business Academy, which is a collaborative network of executives/academics who publish pre-eminent new paradigm business literature.

He has served on numerous non-profit boards including The Gorbachev Foundation, Institute of Transpersonal Psychology, State of the World Forum, and the Center for Earth Concerns. He is a prolific writer and he is the author of a college textbook on nuclear energy, Profiles in Power and a contributor to New Paradigms in Business. An expert in emerging technologies, Rinaldo was co-founder of the nation's first pay cable television operation, CEO Of Universal Subscription Television and CEO of the Red Rose Collection, the sole distributor of Mother Theresa's personally endorsed biographical motion picture.

Rinaldo was raised in a traditional Italian-American family where the Italian traditions and values were emphasized. His grandmother lived in their family home. One of the values that we discussed in our conversation was his father's emphasis on "always honoring the Brutocao name". Everything he does in life he remembers the importance of keeping his word to his father to "honor the Brutocao name" in all his actions.

In his present role, he recently wrote an article entitled, "The Global Family's "Business". In this article, he notes that family businesses need not only to look at the health of their own businesses but to the vitality of the global economic system as well. He points out that family businesses have many opportunities to participate in the global arena but can also do many things "good" for the planet and humankind.

The Italian American Lawyers Assn.

The Italian American Lawyers Assn. (IALA) is now in its 27th year as a Los Angeles-area bar association. It is known for its outstanding speakers and serves authentic Italian meals at the meetings. Early in 1977, the five lawyers and one judge set to establish this organization of Italian American lawyers. They began by scanning a directory for lawyers with Italian-sounding names, and a number of Italians in Los Angeles and Orange counties received a letter inviting them to an organizational meeting on April 17, 1977 at the Beverly Hills home of Paul Caruso. Between 40 and 50 lawyers attended that meeting. The IALA was born.

On July 20, 1977, the first "regular" meeting of the association was held at Casa Italiana, located north of Chinatown. The meetings are still held there today. Caruso was drafted as president. Annual events include the installation ball, the "Gaelic and Garlic Night" held in conjunction with the Irish American Bar Assn., "A Night With the Supreme Court" featuring members of the California state's high court, and "Marco Polo Night" held jointly with the Southern California Chinese Lawyers Assn. and the Japanese American Bar Assn.

Over the years, this organization has given its' members significant opportunities to advance their careers through a number of professional, educational, and networking activities with leading members in the legal profession. The Association also offers a Scholarship Program for deserving students.

National Italian American Bar Association

The National American Italian American Bar Association is a nonprofit, nonpartisan corporation, founded in 1983 to advance the interests of the Italian-American legal community and to improve the administration of justice. NIABA members include judges, law professors, law students and attorneys in both private and public sectors. A Board of Directors elected by the members governs the association.

The organization communicates the views of its members to federal and state officials on matters of common concern in order to improve the administration of justice. It also regularly honors those who have made major contributions to the advancement of the law. It also conducts legal seminars on a wide range of legal topics, covering timely criminal and civil issues important to lawyers in the private and public sectors and works with American and Italian universities in promoting educational programs in Italy for American attorneys, as well as an international exchange program for law students in Italy and the United States.

NIABA also hosts exchanges between members of the Italian and American legal systems to foster better understanding and cooperation on issues that affect both nations. NIABA has also established a Judicial Selection Commission to assist qualified Italo-American lawyers in receiving appointments to the Federal and State benches.

The Justinian Society

The Justinian Society was founded in 1935 by forty-seven attorneys of Italian-Americans in Philadelphia The Justinian Society's mission is to foster a spirit of good fellowship, maintain the honor and dignity of the legal profession, perform civic duties, administer justice, and promote the study of law for it's Italian-American members.

The Society has implemented several committees to better serve Italian-American jurists, barristers, and the community at large. These committees include, the Anti-Defamation Committee, Long-Range Planning Committee, Public Offices Committee, Membership Committee, Scholarship Committee, History Committee and Continuing Legal Education Committee.

The Anti-Defamation Committee serves to eradicate prejudice that may exist against Italian-Americans in the legal profession. This Committee is concerned with displays of negative imaging and stereotyping of Italian-Americans and promotes a positive image of members of the Society as well as responds to attacks, which portray our members and the Italian-American legal community in an unfavorable light because of their ethnicity.

Each year, the Justinian Society awards two scholarships for law related studies. The Jules Fioravanti Scholarship is awarded annually to a graduate of LaSalle

University, my old school, who is planning to attend law school. This scholarship was named after a former chancellor, who is now deceased, of the Society. The second scholarship is open to law students within our region. The Society is also actively involved in the Philadelphia Bar Association and contributes to the Philadelphia Bar Foundation. In addition, The Society promotes the election of its qualified members on the board of governors as well as other major positions within the Philadelphia Bar Association.

The Society also holds quarterly luncheons honoring members of the bench and bar as well as members of our community, and annual golf outing, the joint sponsorship with the Criminal Justice Section of the Bar Association of the Cesare Beccaria Award, and the Christmas Party which is the best attended event of the year.

These are just a few examples of the Italian-American educational and professional organizations that are available to assist the Italian-American community in the United States. If you have not yet engaged in their services, and have a need, I would.

PART III

Remenbering the Lessons of the Past

17

Lessons from our Immigrant Relatives

There are significant lessons that we can learn from the immigrants that built our Italian-American neighborhoods. These lessons are not lessons just for Italian-Americans but for all who are raising children in this very complex, fast paced electronic new world.

As we have seen in this book, our parents have given us a strong foundation of values and traditions to treasure and pass on for many generations to come. But some of these lessons may be lost as we go through the rapid changes that are taking place in our society today. As our neighborhoods change and as we become more dispersed, some of these practices and traditions are now becoming lost.

Doing the research for the book, has given me a chance to refocus on some of these practice, traditions, values and to identify some of the more important lessons to keep in mind when raising our children. At the risk of being consider old fashioned, I have listed some of these lessons in this section of the book. I believe that each of these is timeless and that we may consider how to improve in these areas. In some cases, our immigrant relatives did a much better job then we are.

LESSON #1: EARLIER RESPONSIBLY FOR OUR CHILDREN

Our parents raised us in a community where we where taught very early the importance of accepting responsibility. From their emphasis on our working at an early age, even if it were a part time job, to volunteering, or doing chores at home or school or church. Early responsibility was emphasized everywhere in the community.

When I reviewed the lives of the people who were successful in researching this book, they all had one thing in common. They worked when they were young. They learned responsibility early in their life and they all emphasized that this was a major reason for their success. I have no doubt that if you expand this survey even further, you will find that early responsibility in life is a key factor in determining future success.

There seemed to be a basic law in the Italian-American community: teach individual responsibility early and reinforce it in so many ways. In our home, we were expected to get a job when we were a teenager, do chores around the house, and take care of younger children. In the parish school, we were given chores like clearing the classroom or even gardening. The parish also assigned us volunteering assignments to help the poor. Everywhere we turned there were assignments that were expected of us.

Today, the Italian-American community is trying to fill some of this void through some of the organizations that you have read about in this book. Through some of the programs they are providing opportunities for children to learn early responsibility and they are rewarding children and parents for teaching this value. However, as with almost everything in life, more is needed. Outside the Italian-American organizations, the opportunity for improvement is the greatest. As all of these lessons, this is not an Italian-American issue.

It would be terrific if there would be more opportunities for teenagers to have part-time and summer jobs. I remember in my neighborhood when most of my classmates were going to a job after school and it gave us a sense of pride and responsibility. I do not know one teenager today that has a part-time job. Many of the children in South Philadelphia learned their business and entrepreneurial skills by working with their father in the store or on the pushcart in the neighborhood. They saw the customers and learned how to buy fresh meat and interact with customers and vendors. There is little opportunity today to actually see what your parents actually do.

When my children were young, I was a management consultant and I traveled all over the world consulting to large corporations. This required that I fly on airplanes each week. My wife would take me to the airport each Monday morning with the children in the car and drop me off for my air flights. One day, we were in a Parent's Night at school with my six-year-old son and the teacher asked my six year old what I did for a living. He told the whole room full of teachers, parents, and students that I was an airline pilot. All he saw was me dropped off at the airport each Monday morning. He assumed I flew the plane.

Giving these children jobs as teenagers would be such a good start in life. Getting back to basics and teaching them early responsibilities even if it is only chores to start.

Work with your school or religious organizations to create volunteer programs for them at an early age. This will all go a long way to set the foundation to help your child in the later stages of his/her life. Our immigrant parents proved it.

LESSON #2: APPRECIATE YOUR HERITAGE

In this age of many-cultures, it is easy to lose sight of ones own identity. However, as I researched this book, I found a resurgence of interest from adult Italian-Americans all over the United States. There are many adult Italian-Americans who want to learn more about the heritage and their traditions. The festivals that you have read about in this book, both the religious and those that are just for fun, are experiencing record high attendance.

Many of the organizations that I mention in the book have memberships at record highs also. There is a greater appreciation emerging of people wanting to know more about their roots and their history. More people then ever are interested in their family lineage. Just get on the internet and see the number of sites that are devoted to Italians-Americans tracing their family background.

It would be exciting if, as a parent, you would help your Italian-American children learn more about their heritage while they are young. Excite them to the traditions and the superstitions noted in this book for example while they are young and can enjoy it rather then waiting until they are older and have to learn for themselves when they show interest later in life.

Create memories for them around the Christmas, Easter, and New Years Holidays so that when they grow up they can share those same memories with you that I now have with my parents.

You don't have to be Italian to celebrate these traditions. We have a big heart and have plenty to share. Many non-Italian Catholics that I know, for example, celebrate the Christmas Eve dinner.

The Italian-American organizations in the United States are doing a terrific job in keeping the heritage alive and, if you are interested, please consider joining these organizations listed in the book. There are even new organizations for younger people so they are not just for "old men who play bocce" anymore.

LESSON # 3: ADDITIONAL MENTORS IN THE COMMUNITY HELP CHILDREN

In our neighborhood there were a number of mentors for a child to look up to and admire. There were a number of children who did not have a father or they had a bad father. Now, if there where no other options in the community, the child may be lost and he/she had little chance of growing up as a productive, caring adult. In South Philadelphia, we were lucky. We had options. We were on a first name relationship with the local priest, the policeman, the fireman, the garage mechanic, the bank executive and many more people in the area who could be mentors.

Some of these children were taken into foster homes by families who cared for them as if they were their own. They attended the local parish school and were embraced by the parish as part of the larger community. Others attended the neighborhood orphanage. While they were not part of the parish or the local community, the resources of both were used to support the orphanage. Members would volunteer routinely and on holidays. People would develop relationships with the children to help where they could.

Other mentors included many adults the school children came in contact throughout the day including the teachers, the coaches, and the shopkeepers. The priests and the nuns were dedicated to the religious order and therefore their time was devoted to the children and they were available almost any time the children needed them. There is a significant advantage to attending a religious school and getting the added attention of these dedicated professional teachers.

In our present neighborhoods, access is missing to these types of people. With the de-emphasis, various clubs, organizations, schools, and universities are trying to pick up the slack and provide some to help in this area.

In the Italian-American community many of the organizations that we talk about in this book are tying to provide this access to young Italian-Americans and they are a source for some of these mentors. You have read about some of these examples in this book. However many more Italian American mentors are needed.

In the community, at large, much more needs to be done. I do not believe that the local communities are living up to their responsibilities to assist the families in this area. For example, the local teaches should be held to a "code of responsibilities" as a teacher in the local school district. He/She is a role model to their student and should be held to a standard or expectations on how they should conduct themselves with the younger children in the neighborhood. Like it or not, the students look up to them and admire them.

The local government should also assess the people in its employ that come in contact with children in the neighborhood as well and again develop the same "code of responsibilities" for engaging with the children in the community. This again would help the parents in raising the children by providing good role models in their community to emulate. These steps could go a long way in bringing back the neighborhood mentors that we have lost for our children.

LESSON #4: REBUILD/STRENGTHEN YOUR FAMILY TIES; THE GOVERNMENT IS NOT THE ANSWER

There where a number of times when in the Italian-American community when a family was in financial need. Examples included a loss of a job, grandparents or other relatives who were poor and needed a home, or a family member's illness or death. In these cases, the Italian-American families and their communities banded together to take care of each other in these times of need. There are numerous examples where they worked together as individuals or through their own organizations to provide assistance to those that needed help.

From the beginning when the early immigrants started the first organizations to help the Italians assimilate into America, the Italian-Americans have banded together to help each other in times of need.

In South Philadelphia, many of the homes were populated by at least three generations, if not four and the family took in needy relatives. The family was enriched by the experience. For example, the children grew up leaning much more about their history and their traditions from their grandparent.

That is not to say that government does not provide a role. But too much reliance on the government is also a bad thing as well. The immigrants were a self-reliant group of people that relied on their family first and their friends second. They relied on their country folks next. The story of how they banded together and created the service organizations they needed in a time of trouble for their people is remarkable.

Our families can be an important support system and, over the years, many of us have lost sight of the how important our family really can be to us and to our children.

Lesson #5 Children Need Love and Boundaries more than Possessions

Our family and our neighbors were very poor but we were very happy. Our parents were very strict and we knew where our boundaries were. We did not like it but in the end it turned out that they were right and it was the best for us. Our parents did not try to be our friends or try to understand why we did what we did.

They just told us what was right and what was wrong and we were not to do the wrong thing again. It was such a black and white world at that time. The rules were very simple to follow and you knew the consequences for breaking them.

We cherished every thing that we owned and that was very little. I wish children of today were taught to look past the possessions they receive as gifts and feel the love that is behind the gifts that are given to them. Because we received so few gifts, we felt the love behind them in such a significant way and it was such a wonderful feeling. I wish they could share that feeling today. What would our immigrant forefathers say if they saw us raising our children today? Would they think that we have complicated the process?

I would leave you in this book with two thoughts. One is that you should call your family members and reunite. Secondly, you should start some Italian family traditions of your own today. Family bonds are strong and the memories run deep and the history that unites us is something that we will remember for a very long time.

These are lessons for all of us.

About the Author

Joseph J. Bonocore was born and raised Italian-American in South Philadelphia.

He is a member of a number of Italian-American national and community organizations including the National Italian American Foundation, Il Cenacolo and The Silicon Valley Italian Executive Council.

Joe is the author of Commanding Communications: Navigating Emerging Trends in Telecommunications, a book on the communications industry released by John Wiley & Sons in January 2001. The book was also reprinted in Chinese in 2003.

Joe is the Founder, Chairman and CEO of Impresa Technologies, Inc. Impresa Technologies, Inc. is an operating company that provides a variety of investing and consulting services to its corporate clients around the world. He is also the President and CEO of Bonocore Technology Partners, LLC, a technology consulting organization and a Consultant with DiamondCluster International, a strategy advisory firm.

Joe is the former Founder and Chairman and CEO Eclipse Networks, a national next generation network systems integration company. He also held a number of additional senior management positions in the technology sector over the past 30 years. Prior to founding Eclipse Networks, he was Partner and National Industry Director of KPMG's communications industry practices.

Joe joined KPMG in 1995 when KPMG acquired the San Francisco Consulting Group (SFCG), of which he was the President. At SFCG he managed the firm's sale and subsequent merger with KPMG.

Before joining SFCG, Joe was President and CEO of NYNEX DPI—a NYNEX owned global software and systems-integration Company providing systems solutions to the telecommunications industry.

Other positions Joe has held include Managing Partner, West Coast Consulting, Coopers & Lybrand, LLP (C&L), Finance Manager, General Electric Company, and 1st Lieutenant, U.S. Army, Field Artillery. He has a B.S. Degree in Business from LaSalle University, Philadelphia, PA. He is also a member of Beta Gamma Sigma which is a academic business honorary society.

He is a well respected member of the Communications Industry Community and a frequent speaker at many of the key industry conferences. He also writes on a variety of issues and trends affecting the communications industry.

Joe has been a guest lecturer at the Wharton School of the University of Pennsylvania. He is also a guest lecturer at Stanford University and the University of San Francisco.

He is a member of the Board of Trustees at the University of San Francisco. He is also on the USF School of Business Advisory Board and Chairs their Telecommunications Advisory Board.

978-0-595-35721-5
0-595-35721-0